STAND
on the
WORD
Study Guide

MATTHEW

THE KING AND HIS KINGDOM

A 21-Day Journey through the Word

with Tony Perkins

FAMILY RESEARCH COUNCIL
SINCE 1983

FIDELIS PUBLISHING ®

ISBN: 979-8-9924-1868-2

Matthew: The King and His Kingdom
A Stand on the Word Study Guide

Content contributor: Dr. Kenyn Cureton
Cover design: Diana Lawrence
Copyediting and interior typesetting: Lisa Parnell

Order at www.faithfultext.com for a significant discount.
Email info@fidelispublishing.com to inquire about bulk purchase discounts.

Fidelis Publishing, LLC Winchester, VA • Nashville, TN
www.fidelispublishing.com

Manufactured in the United States of America

10 9 8 7 6 5 4 3 2 1

Contents

Matthew: An Introduction

Welcome to the Stand on the Word Study Guide on Matthew! First, let's set the stage for our move into the New Testament and its first book. Some 400 years had passed since there was a word from God to His people. There were, however, other writings during this 400–year period, including the fourteen books of the Apocrypha. You can find these books today online or in print in the Catholic Bible, placed there in the Catholic Canon of Scripture at the Council of Trent in AD 1546. We do not include them in our Bibles because

1. They were not included in the Hebrew Old Testament and never recognized by the Jewish people as a part of the Old Testament,
2. The Jewish historian Josephus rejected them,
3. Jesus never quoted from any of the fourteen books, and
4. All of the early church leaders did not place the books into the canon of Scripture.

I've read the books, and it's certainly good extracurricular reading; they are not, however, in the canon of our Scriptures, nor should they be treated as such.

It is also important to note some of the history from this 400-year period. In our earlier Stand on the Word journey, we have addressed much of the following. For the benefit of those who are new, however, let's briefly review the historical and prophetic landscape. In 330 BC, Alexander the Great conquered Persia. And between 280 BC and 200 BC, there was the Greek translation of the Old Testament known as the Septuagint. Then in 167 BC, Antiochus IV "Epiphanes" defiled the temple. We read about this ruler especially in Daniel's prophecy, specifically in chapters 7, 8, and 11. Then from 165 BC to 63 BC was the Maccabean period, where we saw the revolt of the Maccabees throwing off Antiochus IV. And for that period of time, the Jews were free again. However, in 63 BC, they came under Roman occupation.

Next let's dive into some of the particulars about the Gospel according to Matthew. It was written by Matthew, a tax collector or publican, who worked with the Roman authorities to collect the taxes. Consequently, the Jews despised Matthew as being a turncoat. However, Matthew responded to the call of Jesus and in fact introduced others to Jesus (see Matt. 9:9–13). Other than the initial encounter we see in this passage and the fact that he was listed among the Twelve, we read nothing else about Matthew.

Matthew's Gospel was most likely written around AD 50–60. It is evident that his Gospel was written before the destruction of Jerusalem occurred in AD 70. Each of the Gospels has a different focus, a different audience. Matthew's Gospel was written to the Jewish community to answer their questions about Jesus. Questions like, "Was He the Messiah predicted in the Old Testament?" Well,

Matthew answered that by directing his readers to several places in the Old Testament prophecies regarding the Messiah and precisely how Jesus fulfilled those prophecies. As we will see in our first study of Matthew 1–2, Matthew pointed to five prophecies. Just an interesting note: Matthew is the only Gospel writer that used the word *church* as a description of those who follow Jesus.

How to Get the Most from the Study Guide

While the study guide offers spiritual insights and applications, the real impact comes from the words of Scripture, which is the Word of God. Please read the selected text for the day in your own Bible. God's Word is "living and powerful" (Heb. 4:12). The Spirit of God uses His Word to change your life. Nothing else can do that. So before reading the daily commentary, read God's Word!

In fact, here are five habits to cultivate as you approach God's Word each day:

1. *Read it through:* Don't skip around. Read the entire selection of Scripture. If you are pressed for time, please read the Bible before you read the study guide notes. So read it through.
2. *Think it over:* Meditate on it. Let it marinate in your mind. If you can, take notes. We provide a notes page at the end of each day. Think it over.
3. *Pray it in:* Personalize the Scripture. Turn the verse that speaks to you into a prayer and then pray it into your life. Ask God what you need to do in response. This leads to the next habit.
4. *Live it out:* Consider ways to apply what God is revealing to you and ways you can obey Him. Put His Word into

practice. Make it a part of who you are, how you think, how you speak, and how you behave toward God and other people. In other words, take God's Word and live it out.

5. *Pass it on:* Don't keep it to yourself. People are in your life who need the same truth God has spoken to you in His Word. Share it. Pass it on.

About Stand on the Word

Stand on the Word is a ministry of Family Research Council, whose mission is to serve in the kingdom of God by championing faith, family, and freedom in public policy and in the culture from a biblical worldview. The purpose of Stand on the Word is to lay the foundation for a biblical worldview through daily reading and application of God's Word. For the daily journey, we have created a chronologically prioritized reading plan through the entire Bible that can be accessed at frc.org/Bible, by texting the word *Bible* to 67742, or by downloading the Stand Firm app.

Roman Empire by the Birth of Jesus

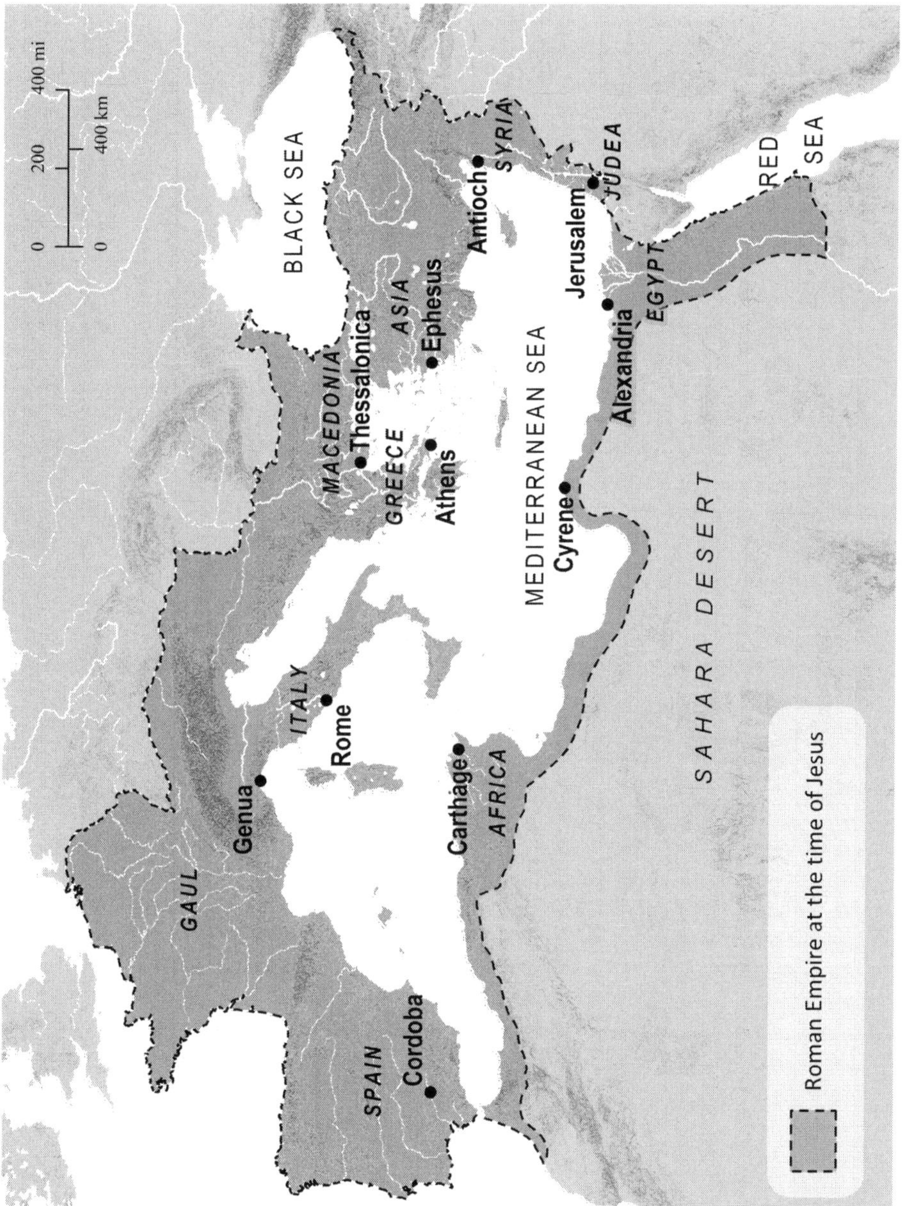

— Day 1 —

Today's Reading: Matthew 1–2

Verse of the Day

> "Now the birth of Jesus Christ was as follows: After His mother Mary was betrothed to Joseph, before they came together, she was found with child of the Holy Spirit.
>
> — *Matthew 1:23*

Please read the entire Scripture selection in your own Bible and highlight or underline verses that stand out to you before you read the observations and engage the questions below.

Today we study Matthew 1–2. Our key verse is found in Matthew 1:23: "'Behold, the virgin shall conceive and bear a son, and they shall call his name Immanuel' (which means, God with us)." You'll notice that this begins with a genealogy, sort of like those you find in the Old Testament (OT). Let's start with verse 1, "The book of the genealogy of Jesus Christ, the Son of David, the Son of Abraham." The Greek word for "genealogy" is *geneseos*, which literally means "Genesis." I find it interesting that this "book of the Genesis of Jesus Christ" opens the New Testament (NT).

What follows is a lot of names connected by "begot." Some may not find genealogies all that exciting, but today there is actually a heightened interest in genealogy, ancestry, and lineage. In other words, people want to know where they came from and who they are related to in the past so that their sense of personal identity can be more informed in the present. In fact, there are a couple of well-known but rival companies who claim to take your DNA sample and tell you where your ancestors came from, at least in a general sense by geographical percentage. You have likely seen the "Ancestry DNA" or "23 and Me" commercials. It is big business. In fact, as of 2025, one in five Americans (21 percent) has taken a DNA test.[1] That is more than 69 million. In 2019, the number was 26 million, so interest has grown. Also there was a show on TLC called "Who Do You Think You Are?" It followed the genealogical searches of American pop-culture celebrities. During the course of the show, the celebrities discovered unknown details about themselves and their families while researching their ancestry with the help of historians and genealogical experts. Part of the reason for this interest may be that there are so many broken homes and blended families. Plus, people are on the move. According to *Forbes*, citing census data, 12.6 percent of Americans moved in the past few years. That's 41.5 million people.[2] Perhaps because of the rootlessness that comes from fractured families and people moving there has been a renewed interest in ancestry.

Interestingly, the Jews highly value their genealogy. Back in the days of Ezra, waves of Jewish refugees from their exile in Babylon were gradually returning to the promised land, and some presented themselves as priests. However, they couldn't verify their genealogy and therefore could not prove that they were descendants of Levi. Consequently, they lost their status in society and lost their opportunity for livelihood as priests. More importantly, God Himself was focused on genealogy and ancestry. The twelve tribes came from twelve descendants of Jacob. Then when those tribes came out of Egypt and into the promised land, they were allotted land by tribe. As mentioned above, the tribe of Levi was singled out to provide for the priesthood through Aaron's lineage. Additionally, the tribe of Judah was singled out to provide for the monarchy through David's lineage.

In today's terms, a person without a verified genealogy in the biblical world was like a modern American without a birth certificate, Social Security number, driver's license, passport, and so on. You are suspect without that identifying information. When it comes to the story of Jesus, you'll remember that Jesus's ancestry was questioned almost from the beginning. Whispers in the streets of Nazareth were about the paternity of Jesus. Mary and Joseph were engaged to be married, she was found with child, and Joseph was not the father. You can almost sense the scorn and ridicule in the voices of the Pharisees in John 8:39 when they said, "Abraham is our father" then added in verse 41, "We were not born of fornication." Then to further cast aspersions on Jesus's parentage, they said of him in verse 48 that He was a Samaritan and had a demon. In other words, Jesus, You are a half breed, a mixed-race mongrel who has no clue who His father is. There was a question mark over the birth of the Lord Jesus that required a statement of His genealogy.

Under the leadership of the Spirit and writing predominately for a Jewish audience, Matthew began his Gospel with a genealogy, selectively reporting the ancestry and lineage of Jesus Messiah. While first-century Jews pointed to their ancestry as a matter of pride, position and prestige, Matthew arranged his genealogy of Jesus for his own purposes. He begins with the two most significant ancestors that anchor the ancestry of Jesus: David and Abraham. Obviously, Abraham was the "founding father" of the Jewish people and David was the greatest king, through whom came Messiah.

Yet as we proceed, all sorts of humanity are represented. In fact, five women are listed in this genealogy, which was surprising because Hebrew genealogy was patriarchal. Their inclusion as well as their stories speak to the grace, mercy, forgiveness, and redemption of God. Several of these women had serious baggage, to put it lightly. Two of the women were Gentiles, Rahab and Ruth. Rahab was the harlot or the prostitute who hid the spies in Jericho. Then there was Tamar who played the role of a harlot and had a child by her father-in-law, who thought she was a harlot, and therefore he had a little bit more explaining to do than she did. Then there was the one listed as the wife of Uriah. She wasn't even mentioned by name, but of course we know that was Bathsheba, who committed adultery with David and who bore Solomon. Finally, there was Mary, the mother of Jesus. I believe Matthew included some of these women under the Spirit's guidance to communicate the message that by the grace of God even broken people can play a part in God's glorious plan to redeem the world.

But that's not all. In verse 4 we find Amminadab, who was a slave and one of the ancestors of the One who came to set us free. Down in verse 8, we have Asa, a composer of songs, in the genealogy of the One who came to give us a song in our hearts. Then in verse 12, we find Zerubbabel, whom God used to rebuild the temple, part of the ancestry of our Lord who said, "Destroy this temple [meaning His body], and in three days I will raise it up" (John 2:19). In Matthew 1:13 we find Eliakim, one of the prophets of the OT, a predecessor of Him who came to be Prophet of Promise (Deut. 18:15–18). Then in Matthew 1:14 we find priests Zadok and Eliud, ancestors of the One who came to be our great High Priest! Consequently, when we look into the forty-two generations of the genealogy of Jesus, we find all sorts of humanity represented:

Jews, Gentiles, women, men, slaves, kings, prostitutes, prophets, and priests. It is as though the Spirit of God is saying through Matthew, "If anyone could be a part of His ancestry, anyone can be a part of His family today by faith." So this genealogy represents God's promise that whoever you are, whatever your background, or whatever your past might be, if these sort of people can be numbered among the ancestors of Jesus according to the flesh, then we can belong to the descendants of Jesus by the Spirit. God used all sorts of people to accomplish His divine purposes, and He can use us—if we are willing.

All that said, I must point out that while the Lord Jesus has a genealogy, He cannot be explained fully by this genealogy. After all of the "begots" from verses 2–15, we come to Matthew 1:16, where Matthew, led by the Spirit of God with laser-like precision, said, "Joseph the husband of Mary, of whom was born Jesus who is called Christ." So this genealogy of Jesus ends by pointing to where the next verses begin, with the virgin birth. Let's continue in Matthew 1:18–23:

> Now the birth of Jesus Christ was as follows: After His mother Mary was betrothed to Joseph, before they came together, she was found with child of the Holy Spirit. Then Joseph her husband, being a just man, and not wanting to make her a public example, was minded to put her away secretly. But while he thought about these things, behold, an angel of the Lord appeared to him in a dream, saying, "Joseph, son of David, do not be afraid to take to you Mary your wife, for that which is conceived in her is of the Holy Spirit. And she will bring forth a Son, and you shall call His name JESUS, for He will save His people from their sins."

> So all this was done that it might be fulfilled which was spoken by the Lord through the prophet, saying: "Behold, the virgin shall be with child, and bear a Son, and they shall call His name Immanuel," which is translated, "God with us."

Note that the name Jesus means "savior" or "deliverer," and it matches His mission: "you shall call His name JESUS, for He will save His people from their sins" (v. 21). That's why the human genealogy of Jesus ultimately falls short. To be our Savior, Jesus had to be conceived of the Holy Spirit and born of a virgin to have a sinless nature. That is a fundamental of the Christian faith because it is the only way Jesus became the sinless sacrifice, to satisfy the demands of a Holy God because of our sin. That's why Jesus wasn't the physical son of Joseph, though He shared Joseph's home and his humanity. He had to be without sin. Consequently, Jesus was not the son of Joseph but the Son of God—"Immanuel," God with us.

Two more thoughts before we move on to chapter 2. The first is that Matthew is careful to point out how Jesus is the fulfillment of OT prophecy, quoting Isaiah 7:14. That is a thread that runs throughout his Gospel and was meaningful to a predominately Jewish audience. Secondly, I feel compelled to commend Joseph. Most of the focus is on Mary in the events surrounding the birth of Jesus, and rightly so, but Joseph is the "forgotten man" of the Christmas story. Have you noticed that Joseph is even left out of some of the manger scenes? Yet we read here that he was not only a just man, but he was also compassionate. As a carpenter, he depended on the community to keep him in business, and the news that his fiancée was expecting, and he was not the biological father, could cause not only embarrassment but also threaten his livelihood. To his credit, he was more concerned about Mary's reputation, so he decided to end the betrothal privately. Yet when the angel of the Lord told him to go through with the marriage, he obeyed. We read in Matthew 1:24–25, "Then Joseph, being aroused from sleep, did as the angel of the Lord commanded him and took to him his wife, and did not know her till she had brought forth her firstborn Son. And he called His name JESUS." Joseph's obedience was complete.

In Matthew 2:2–12, we have the visit of the magi or wise men to Bethlehem, the place of Messiah's birth in fulfillment of Scripture (see Mic. 5:2), then in Matthew 2:13–15 we have Joseph's second dream with angelic instructions to flee Herod by moving to Egypt, which Matthew pointed out was the fulfillment of Scripture (see Hos. 11:1). In Matthew 2:16–18, we have the report of wicked Herod's slaughter of the innocent children in his attempt to kill Jesus, which Matthew pointed out was the fulfillment of Scripture (see Jer. 31:15), and in Matthew 2:19–23, finally the little family's return to the land of Israel, once again prompted by an angelic messenger through Joseph's dream—and specifically to Nazareth, yet again via a dream, which Matthew again pointed out was in fulfillment of Scripture (see Isa. 11:1). Hopefully, you are seeing the pattern here. Matthew repeatedly told us that everything significant about the life and ministry of Jesus was in fulfillment of prophecy.

Before we conclude our study, I want to point out a few significant things about the visit of the wise men. Let's look at Matthew 2:1–2, "Now after Jesus was born in Bethlehem of Judea in the days of Herod the king, behold, wise men from the East came to Jerusalem, saying, 'Where is He who has been born King of the Jews? For we have seen His star in the East and have come to worship Him.'" We all know the Christmas song "We Three Kings," but these men were not kings but "wise men." The Greek word is *magoi*, or magi. They were a priestly class of philosopher-astrologers from the "Orient," or the east—probably from Persia or the current-day region of Iraq or Iran. As such, they would have had knowledge of Daniel and his prophecies of the coming Messiah (e.g., Dan. 9:24–26). Also, they likely had knowledge of Balaam, an internationally known seer who came from the region of the Euphrates in the east, and his prophecy in Numbers 24:17:

> "I see Him, but not now;
> I behold Him, but not near;
> A Star shall come out of Jacob;
> A Scepter shall rise out of Israel."

When they saw "his star," they set out on their journey, which took time. This may explain why the wise men were not present when Jesus was born (like the shepherds were) because the Greek word for "child" in Matthew 2:8–9 indicates they came later. There is a lot of debate about the star they witnessed. Some point to a convergence of the planets, a supernova or some other star, basically a natural occurrence in the heavens. However, I believe this was a supernatural manifestation of the glory of God in the heavens, the same glory that shone round about the shepherds in Luke 2. This heavenly glory appeared (Matt. 2:7), and it moved as we read in verses 9–10: "When they heard the king, they departed; and behold, the star which they had seen in the East went before them, till it came and stood over where the young Child was. When they saw the star, they rejoiced with exceedingly great joy." This "star" led these wise men directly to Jesus.

Filled with joy, these wise men had come to worship Him (v. 2), and we read about the extravagant gifts they brought in verse 11:

"And when they had come into the house, they saw the young Child with Mary His mother, and fell down and worshiped Him. And when they had opened their treasures, they presented gifts to Him: gold, frankincense, and myrrh."

How can we apply this? What can we bring the Lord Jesus? First, we can recognize His dominion by giving Him our gold, our wealth. He is the King of kings and Lord of lords, and He owns it all, yet He only requires a tithe and offerings given out of a grateful heart. We should offer Him a portion of our wealth to advance His kingdom. Second, we should recognize His deity by offering Him our worship, which is symbolized by frankincense. The shepherds bowed, the wise men bowed, and we should bow. As the carol says, "O come let us adore Him." We should bring Jesus our worship. Third, because myrrh speaks of His sacrificial death, we can honor that by giving Him our witness. We can let the world know He died for us. Remember, it is the cross—not the cradle—that's the central symbol of Christianity. Yet thank God for the cradle, the cross, and the crown. Jesus is worthy of our worship!

Questions for Reflection and Discussion

1. Why did Joseph decide to go through with the marriage to Mary (see 1:19–21)?

2. What gifts did the wise men bring the Christ child in chapter 2?
   a. Gold
   b. Frankincense
   c. Myrrh
   d. All of the above

Notes from Today's Reading

Israel During the Time of Jesus

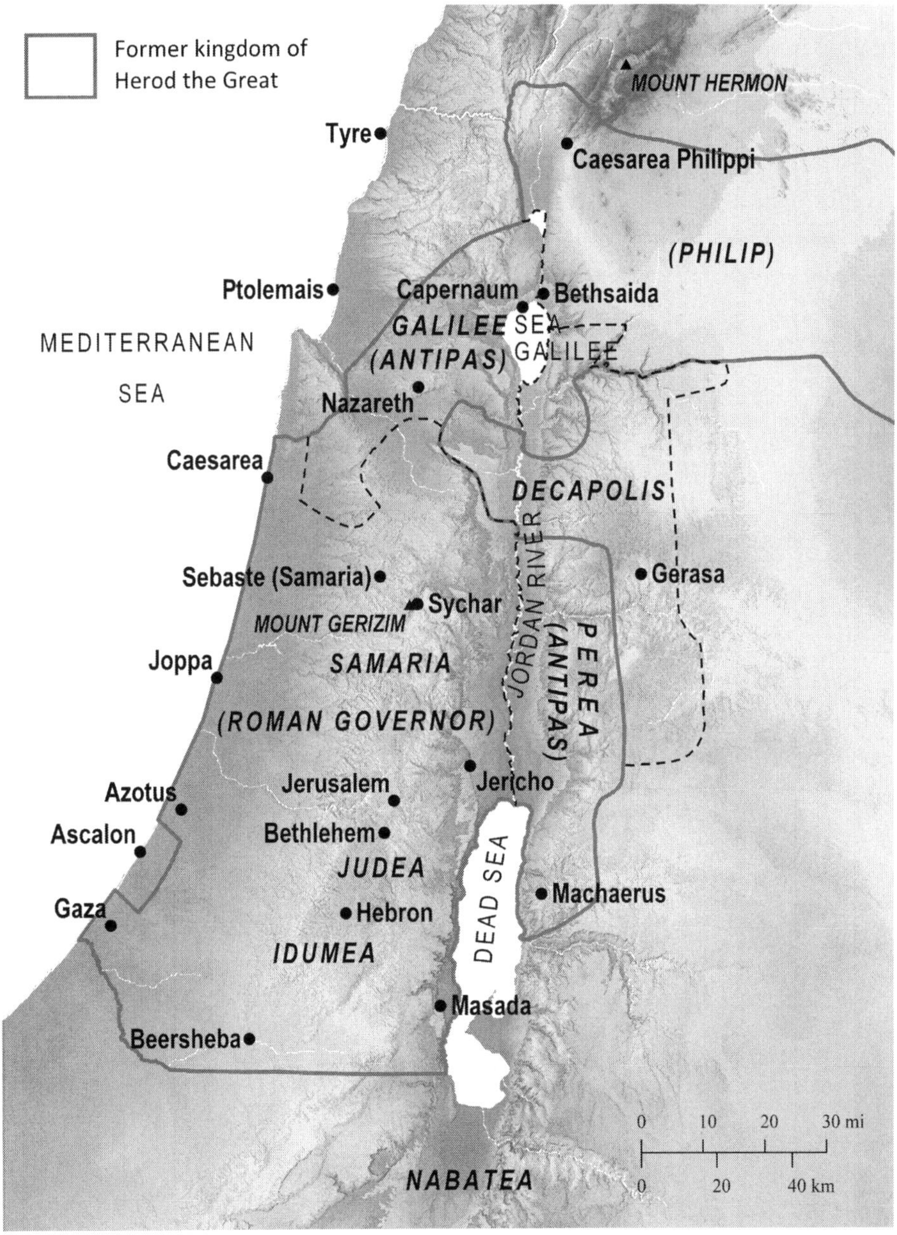

— Day 2 —

Today's Reading: Matthew 3–4

Verse of the Day

> But He answered and said, "It is written, 'Man shall not live by bread alone, but by every word that proceeds from the mouth of God.'"
>
> — *Matthew 4:4*

Please read the entire Scripture selection in your own Bible and highlight or underline verses that stand out to you before you read the observations and engage the questions below.

Today we look at Matthew 3–4. In these chapters we read about the ministry of John the Baptist and the baptism of Jesus, and then we read about the temptation of Jesus, His early preaching, the call of His disciples, and His healing ministry. Our key verse is 4:4: "But He answered and said, 'It is written, "Man shall not live by bread alone, but by every word that proceeds from the mouth of God."'"

In chapter 3, we find John the Baptist, the one who was written about in Malachi as preparing the way. Look at Matthew 3:1–2: "In those days John the Baptist came preaching in the wilderness of Judea, and saying, 'Repent, for the kingdom of heaven is at hand!'" Notice what he called for: repentance, which means in the Greek to change your mind, change your thinking. But a mind or heart change, one that's truly changed, will result in bearing fruit: "Therefore bear fruits worthy of repentance" (v. 8). A changed heart will lead to a changed life.

Look at Matthew 3:13: "Then Jesus came from Galilee to John at the Jordan to be baptized by him." This is the baptism of Jesus. Now go down to verses 16–17: "When He had been baptized, Jesus came up immediately from the water; and behold, the heavens were opened to Him, and He saw the Spirit of God descending like a dove and alighting upon Him. And suddenly a voice came from heaven, saying, 'This is My beloved Son, in whom I am well pleased.'"

Two observations here: (1) The power of the Holy Spirit came upon Jesus as His public ministry began. Our work for the Lord must be empowered by the Holy Spirit. We'll see later in the book of Matthew where Jesus told the disciples to wait in Jerusalem until the power of the Holy Spirit had come upon them. He did that at the ascension. And (2) the power of the Holy Spirit was ignited by the blessing of the Father. I believe that Jesus the Son and God the Father model for us the need for and the power of the affirming words of a Father.

In chapter 4, we see first a season of preparation then a series of temptations. Look at verse 1: "Then Jesus was led up by the Spirit into the wilderness to be tempted by the devil." Now, don't miss this critical detail in this verse: Jesus, the Son of God, a member of the Trinity, was led by the Spirit. I point that out because what we're going to see here throughout the Gospels in Jesus's life is that He is a model for us. He was encountering life for our benefit. We need to learn from Him. And this is a perfect example as we start with the temptations and the testing that came toward Jesus from

Satan. There wasn't a chance that Jesus was going to fail this test, but He modeled for us how we should respond to temptation. Look at Matthew 4:2–6:

> And when He had fasted forty days and forty nights, afterward He was hungry. Now when the tempter came to Him, he said, "If You are the Son of God, command that these stones become bread." But He answered and said, "It is written, 'Man shall not live by bread alone, but by every word that proceeds from the mouth of God.'" Then the devil took Him up into the holy city, set Him on the pinnacle of the temple, and said to Him, "If You are the Son of God, throw Yourself down. For it is written:
>
> 'He shall give His angels charge over you,' and,
> 'In their hands they shall bear you up,
> Lest you dash your foot against a stone.'"

If you paid close attention, you realized that Satan quoted Scripture, and he twisted it.

Let's continue in Matthew 4:7–9, "Jesus said to him, 'It is written again, "You shall not tempt the LORD your God."' Again, the devil took Him up on an exceedingly high mountain, and showed Him all the kingdoms of the world and their glory. And he said to Him, 'All these things I will give You if You will fall down and worship me.'" Notice here that Jesus didn't challenge the assertion that Satan had control over these kingdoms. He still has influence over this world. He will be defeated, but that defeat and the culmination of that defeat is yet to come. Look at verses 10–11: "Then Jesus said to him, 'Away with you, Satan! For it is written, "You shall worship the LORD your God, and Him only you shall serve."' Then the devil left Him, and behold, angels came and ministered to Him." What can we learn here from Jesus and how He resisted the devil? I believe He shows us four elements/aspects of resisting the devil.

The first aspect of resisting the devil is the power of identity. Notice the first thing that Satan challenged or questioned was Jesus's identity. He said, "If You are the Son of God." Remember two significant actions took place in Matthew 3 at the baptism: (1) the anointing of the Holy Spirit—that was the power—and (2) the affirmation by the Father. You see, Jesus knew who He was. He was the Son of God. We need to know who we are in Christ. In Galatians 2:20, Paul said, "I have been crucified with Christ; it is no longer I who live, but Christ lives in me; and the life which I now live in the flesh I live by faith in the Son of God, who loved me and gave Himself for me." Over in 2 Corinthians 5:17, Paul wrote this: "Therefore, if anyone is in Christ, he is a new creation; old things have passed away; behold, all things have become new." We need to know who we are in Christ because Satan is going to come and test us.

The second aspect of resisting the devil is the power of purpose. This is extremely important. Jesus knew His purpose. Look at Luke 4:43: "But He said to them, 'I must preach the kingdom of God to the other cities also, because for this purpose I have been sent.'" Jesus knew His purpose. We must know our purpose. Look at Colossians 3:1–3, "If then you were raised with Christ, seek those things which are above, where Christ is, sitting at the right hand of God. Set your mind on things above, not on things on the earth. For you died, and your life is hidden with Christ in God." We need to know our purpose. Our purpose is to live for the Lord. I love the Westminster Shorter Catechism. The first question in there is, "What is the chief end of man?" Man's chief end is to glorify God and to enjoy Him forever. That's our purpose, to know God and to make Him known.

The third aspect of resisting the devil is the power of the Holy Spirit. Jesus walked in the power of the Holy Spirit. Look at Luke 4:1, "Then Jesus, being filled with the Holy Spirit, returned from the Jordan and was led by the Spirit into the wilderness." We must walk in the power of the Spirit. How do we do that? Well, we receive the Holy Spirit when we're saved. The Holy Spirit comes, and He seals us. He comes and dwells within us. We become the temple of God, the Holy Spirit. But we choose by our habits or our actions what we will be filled with. In Ephesians 5:18 Paul said to "be filled with the Spirit." Look what he wrote in Galatians 5:16: "I say then: Walk in the Spirit, and you shall not fulfill the lust of the flesh." We choose what we will fill our hearts and minds with. And we do that by what we read, what we watch, what we listen to, what we think about. So we need to meditate upon the things of God. We need to be in His Word. That's why this journey through the Bible is so important. And it's encouraging to hear from so many of you how the Word of God has impacted your lives and in many cases marriages and relationships. That is how we become filled with the Holy Spirit—by dwelling in His presence.

The fourth aspect of resisting the devil is the power of the Word. Jesus used the Word. Now don't miss this. He said in Matthew 4:4, "'It is written.'" Notice that Jesus didn't try to reason with Satan. He didn't debate Satan. He didn't try to find common ground with Satan. He simply responded to Him with the Word of God. You and I must know and use the Word of God. And that's why I think there's this effort to try to marginalize the Word of God and take it out of our society. It was taken out of our schools sixty years ago, and our culture is pushing it to the recesses of society. We need to be in the Word of God. Our children need to know the Word of God. Psalm 119:11 says, "Your word I have hidden in my heart,

That I might not sin against You." When that moment of testing comes from Satan, the Word of God will not do you any good if it's in your drawer or on your shelf. It must be in your heart. It must be on your lips.

Years ago, when I was a police officer, I went to a police officer's survival course. We did these different case studies where one learns from mistakes. One of these was from 1986. The FBI had a shootout in Miami that left two agents dead. Five others were wounded. The incident fundamentally changed law enforcement in America, leading to several reforms from communications to ammunition to even the types of weapons that officers carry. But what struck me and remains with me to this day was the story of an agent who routinely placed his gun on the seat of his car, where he could get to it when needed. But in the pursuit of heavily armed bank robbers, his gun became lost in his car, and he didn't have it in the gun battle that ensued. He couldn't find it.

When the temptations of Satan are upon us, we should not be looking for where we put the Word. We don't need to be looking for it at that moment. We need to have a firm grip upon it. It needs to be in our hearts, in our minds, and on our lips to resist the devil and make him flee. We need to know who we are in Christ. We need to know our identity. We must understand and know our purpose in Christ Jesus. We must be filled with and walk in the power of the Spirit, and we must be equipped with and know how to use the Word of God.

Questions for Reflection and Discussion

1. What happened when John baptized Jesus (see 3:13–17)?
   a. The heavens were opened.
   b. The Spirit descended like a dove.

c. A voice from heaven spoke affirmation.
d. All of the above.

2. How did Jesus counter Satan's temptations to sin and deviate from God's mission of the cross (see 4:1–11)?

Notes on Today's Bible Reading

— Day 3 —

Today's Reading: Matthew 5

Verse of the Day

> And seeing the multitudes, He went up on a mountain, and when He was seated His disciples came to Him. Then He opened His mouth and taught them, saying:
>
> — *Matthew 5:1–2*

Please read the entire Scripture selection in your own Bible and highlight or underline verses that stand out to you before you read the observations and engage the questions below.

Today we will look at the opening chapter of the Sermon on the Mount, Matthew 5. Verse 2 is key: "Then He opened His mouth and taught them, saying." The Sermon on the Mount comprises three full chapters. This is the longest discourse of Jesus in the NT. Here in chapter 5, we first find what is called the Beatitudes, which means "supreme blessedness." Now some scholars suggest that the Beatitudes are to the New Testament what the Ten Commandments are to the Old. And I think that's true to the degree that it sets out the standards, the Constitution, if you will, for Kingdom living. The Beatitudes tell us the "what" in so far as what is expected, but they don't tell us the "how." We can't keep these standards any better than they were able to keep the standard of the Ten Commandments in the OT. It describes what the kingdom of God will look like when Jesus returns and reigns. But in the meantime, we should pursue solid principles for living in and through the power of the Holy Spirit. And what we'll see in the NT, in the Gospels, is that the principles for Kingdom living are amplified through Jesus's ministry in both His words and His actions.

Let's begin in Matthew 5:1–2: "And seeing the multitudes, He went up on a mountain, and when He was seated His disciples came to Him. Then He opened His mouth and taught them, saying." Note first the parallel to Moses on the mountain, receiving then delivering the Ten Commandments. Here was Jesus on a mountain like the New Moses in fulfillment of Deuteronomy 18:15–18. Then notice that Jesus took a seat, which was the posture of a rabbi, a teacher.

Jesus grabs our attention from the outset of the Sermon on the Mount with what we call eight paradoxes, which amplify the counterintuitive nature of the kingdom of God. Look at Matthew 5:3: "'Blessed are the poor in spirit, For theirs is the kingdom of heaven." The word *blessed* means happy, supremely blessed. From the start, what we see here is something different about the kingdom of God. And it's radical. It's internal, not external. Notice He said, "poor in spirit." This has nothing to do with material possessions. This is speaking of those who understand their impoverished spiritual state and their need for a Savior. And those who recognize this spiritual poverty and accept Jesus Christ as the One who reconciles them with God will have the kingdom of heaven. It tells us the "what" but not the "how." That comes in the rest of the Gospels.

Let's continue in Matthew 5:4–9:

"Blessed are those who mourn,
For they shall be comforted.
Blessed are the meek,
For they shall inherit the earth.
Blessed are those who hunger and thirst for righteousness,
For they shall be filled.
Blessed are the merciful,
For they shall obtain mercy.
Blessed are the pure in heart,
For they shall see God.
Blessed are the peacemakers,
For they shall be called sons of God.

Again, these are counterintuitive to the culture. The world says be proud, take pride in who you are, but Jesus said in verse 3 to become poor in spirit, be humble before God like a bankrupt beggar. The world says celebrate your sin, but Jesus said in verse 4 to mourn over your sin. The world says be strong, but Jesus said in verse 5 to be meek. The world says be self-sufficient, rely on yourself, and do it yourself, but Jesus said in verse 6 to hunger and thirst, be desperate for Him and His righteousness. The world says show no mercy, but Jesus said in verse 7 to be merciful. The world says be shrewd, even deceptive to get ahead, but Jesus said in verse 8 to be pure, sincere, a straight shooter. The world says disrupt and divide, be a troublemaker, but Jesus said in verse 9 to be a peacemaker.

Let's continue in verses 10–11:

"Blessed are those who are persecuted for righteousness' sake,
For theirs is the kingdom of heaven.

> "Blessed are you when they revile and persecute you, and say all kinds of evil against you falsely for My sake."

Look at the amplifier here: they persecute and make false allegations in statements because of Jesus. From the start to the finish of Jesus's ministry, He warns us that as we follow the King and the ways of the kingdom, we will face opposition and persecution. And we need to make sure it's for the sake of Christ, His Word, His ways, not because of something we do.

Yet notice the response in verse 12: "Rejoice and be exceedingly glad, for great is your reward in heaven, for so they persecuted the prophets who were before you." I have two observations from this verse. The first is that the persecution is on this earth, and the reward is in heaven. The earth is temporal and heaven is eternal. Weigh the two. And secondly, we are not the first. We naturally tend to view the world through our own context, but we need to realize that our context is quite limited. While our life experiences are clearly important and they're helpful, they do not represent the totality of the history of the human race or the world. While what we've seen in our lives is one thing, it doesn't represent what is happening even around the world. There is an increased persecution of Christians. This has been going on for years globally, but it's something that's now happening here in the United States. We've documented this, and you can actually read the report FRC compiled on these attacks on churches if you go to frc.org/church.

Again, this might be new to us, but it's not new. In fact, I highly recommend a book by Dr. Bill Bennett, longtime friend and former Secretary of Education and the Drug Czar, who served under presidents Ronald Reagan and George H. W. Bush. The title of the book is *Tried by Fire: The Story of Christianity's First Thousand Years.*

The history of the church is a story of persecution. We've enjoyed relative peace here in the United States because of the influence of the church, and that influence has been pervasive. But as the church has retreated from its mission, which we'll see in the next few verses, we have seen an increase, once again, in hostility to those who truly follow Jesus Christ and live counter to the culture and to the ways of the world.

The mission of those who follow Jesus Christ is to preserve salt and to guide light. Look at Matthew 5:13: "You are the salt of the earth; but if the salt loses its flavor, how shall it be seasoned? It is then good for nothing but to be thrown out and trampled underfoot by men." We cannot accomplish this mission if we're standing on the sidelines or hiding in our churches. Salt must permeate to be effective. And verses 14–16: "You are the light of the world. A city that is set on a hill cannot be hidden. Nor do they light a lamp and put it under a basket, but on a lampstand, and it gives light to all who are in the house. Let your light so shine before men, that they may see your good works and glorify your Father in heaven."

What is the purpose of our mission? It's not to bring glory and recognition to ourselves but to bring glory to the Father, just as Jesus did. This does not say that the light we shine will be welcomed and appreciated by all. In fact, this is what leads to persecution. But for those whose eyes are opened to the light, they are the ones who will give glory to God because they will be set free. They will know life, and they will have that life abundantly, which Jesus came to bring to us. And so, they will give testimony of Jesus's faithful followers.

The next section moves to Jesus and the law. Look at Matthew 5:17–18: "'Do not think that I came to destroy the Law or the Prophets. I did not come to destroy but to fulfill. For assuredly,

I say to you, till heaven and earth pass away, one jot or one tittle will by no means pass from the law till all is fulfilled." So Jesus did not come to subvert, abrogate, or to annul the law but to establish the law and the prophets. He, in His own conduct and life, kept the law perfectly, and He fulfilled the promise of God through the prophets by providing reconciliation for humans to God. He also took the law from the status of ceremony for community to the very character of a people. Note, this is significant. Keep in mind that the law is an expression of God's unchanging, unfaltering holiness. Therefore, it does not change. But Jesus took it to a new level in the new covenant.

Let's continue in verse 19: "'Whoever therefore breaks one of the least of these commandments, and teaches men so, shall be called least in the kingdom of heaven; but whoever does and teaches them, he shall be called great in the kingdom of heaven." Be sure to take note of this warning about those who teach a message that is counter to the Word of God. James also warned about this in 3:1: "My brethren, let not many of you become teachers, knowing that we shall receive a stricter judgment." I just want you to know that I take this warning quite seriously. I'm prayerful and cautious about what I teach and what I preach, and that includes this journey we're doing through the Bible.

What we find is far from Jesus destroying the law. Remember, He moved it from external rules of constraint to internal righteousness, which is an even more difficult standard to obtain. In fact, it's an impossible standard for humanity but not for God. Look at Matthew 5:21–22: "'You have heard that it was said to those of old, "You shall not murder, and whoever murders will be in danger of the judgment." But I say to you that whoever is angry with his brother without a cause shall be in danger of the judgment. And whoever says to his brother, "Raca!" shall be in danger of the council. But whoever says, "You fool!" shall be in danger of hell fire.'" As we see here, breaking the sixth commandment (see Exod. 20:13; Deut. 5:17) is no longer simply understood as the outward act of murder, but now it also includes the inward attitude of anger, disrespect, and hatred in our hearts.

There is a pattern here. Look next at Matthew 5:27–28: "You have heard that it was said to those of old, 'You shall not commit adultery.' But I say to you that whoever looks at a woman to lust for her has already committed adultery with her in his heart." Consequently, breaking the seventh commandment is no longer the outward act of sexual immorality, including adultery, but also the inward lust and impurity in our hearts. The standard has changed. It's moved from external restraints to internal righteousness, which can only be obtained through forgiveness of our sins through the Lord Jesus Christ by the power of the Holy Spirit.

Notice the drastic actions suggested here as a remedy in Matthew 5:29–30: "'If your right eye causes you to sin, pluck it out and cast it from you; for it is more profitable for you that one of your members perish, than for your whole body to be cast into hell. And if your right hand causes you to sin, cut it off and cast it from you; for it is more profitable for you that one of your members perish, than for your whole body to be cast into hell.'"

This is allegorical. It's not saying that we should pluck out our eyes to keep from looking at the provocative. In fact, if that were the case, given today's culture and what we see happening around us, there'd be a lot of blind people. It means we should take that which brings immorality into our hearts and minds seriously, and we need to get rid of it. Is it television? Is it romance models? Is it the computer? Our phones? Whatever it is, we need to take drastic actions so that we are protecting what is in our hearts and in our minds.

Let's continue in verses 31–32: "'Furthermore it has been said, 'Whoever divorces his wife, let him give her a certificate of divorce.' But I say to you that whoever divorces his wife for any reason except sexual immorality causes her to commit adultery; and whoever marries a woman who is divorced commits adultery." We are going to be discussing marriage and divorce in greater detail later in Matthew. We'll stop here, but be sure to read the rest of the chapter.

Questions for Reflection and Discussion

1. To what did Jesus compare His followers' intended influence and impact (see vv. 13–16)?
   a. Bread and butter
   b. Salt and pepper
   c. Salt and light
   d. None of the above

2. According to Jesus, how are we to treat our enemies (see vv. 43–48)?

Notes on Today's Bible Reading

— Day 4 —

Today's Reading: Matthew 6–7

Verse of the Day

> "But seek first the kingdom of God and His righteousness, and all these things shall be added to you."
>
> — *Matthew 6:33*

Please read the entire Scripture selection in your own Bible and highlight or underline verses that stand out to you before you read the observations and engage the questions below.

Matthew 6–7 cover the call of the Kingdom and answer the question, How do we live in the Kingdom? Our key verse is Matthew 6:33: "'But seek first the kingdom of God and His righteousness, and all these things shall be added to you.'" As we talked about before, the Sermon on the Mount is the longest discourse of Jesus in the Bible. It is all about Kingdom living. As we will see, it is a matter of the heart.

We have a lot of ground to cover today, so let's start in Matthew 6:1–2: "'Take heed that you do not do your charitable deeds before men, to be seen by them. Otherwise you have no reward from your Father in heaven. Therefore, when you do a charitable deed, do not sound a trumpet before you as the hypocrites do in the synagogues and in the streets, that they may have glory from men. Assuredly, I say to you, they have their reward.'"

In the first eighteen verses of chapter 6, we have the three primary religious practices of the Pharisees. These were central to their religion: (1) charitable giving, (2) prayer, and (3) fasting. These are all good practices and a part of our relationship with God when they are done to honor God and not impress people, which was what Jesus took issue with here.

Look at verses 6–8: "'But you, when you pray, go into your room, and when you have shut your door, pray to your Father who is in the secret place; and your Father who sees in secret will reward you openly. And when you pray, do not use vain repetitions as the heathen do. For they think that they will be heard for their many words. 'Therefore do not be like them. For your Father knows the things you have need of before you ask Him.'" Jesus then provided kind of a model or a pattern of a prayer, and notice this is in contrast to the many words He makes reference to in verse 7. Now, this is not something I believe that we should be necessarily praying. This is not a prayer to be repeated. Remember, He just warned against vain repetitions. It is a model and a pattern.

Look at Matthew 6:9–13:

> "In this manner, therefore, pray:
> Our Father in heaven,
> Hallowed be Your name.
> Your kingdom come.
> Your will be done
> On earth as it is in heaven.
> Give us this day our daily bread.
> And forgive us our debts,

As we forgive our debtors.
And do not lead us into temptation,
But deliver us from the evil one.
For Yours is the kingdom and the power and the glory forever. Amen."

There are seven parts or seven petitions in this prayer: Number 1 is praise and glory to the Father. Our prayers should begin with a recognition of the glory that is due to the Father, the creator. Number 2 is a recognition and an invitation for the kingdom of God. God is not going to impose Himself on us. We've got to, as we see here with number 3, yield to the will of God in our personal lives. Number 4 is a request for our daily needs to be met. Number 5 is a request for forgiveness as we forgive others. Number 6 is a request not to be led into temptation. And finally, number 7 is a request for deliverance from the evil one.

Now drop down to verse 19 as we look at another principle of Kingdom living, and that's finances. Matthew 6:19–21 says, "'Do not lay up for yourselves treasures on earth, where moth and rust destroy and where thieves break in and steal; but lay up for yourselves treasures in heaven, where neither moth nor rust destroys and where thieves do not break in and steal. For where your treasure is, there your heart will be also.'" Again, we see that the kingdom of God is about the heart.

Let me ask you this question: Is money evil? Is it bad? No, it's actually absent of any intrinsic moral distinction. It's kind of like fire. It's good for cooking if you're cooking your daily bread but bad if it's used by an arsonist to burn down your house. It's about how we use it, and that is determined by our hearts. Look at verse 24: "'No one can serve two masters; for either he will hate the one and love the other, or else he will be loyal to the one and despise the other. You cannot serve God and mammon.'" It's interesting, in this sermon, Jesus devoted most of His time to discussing prayer. That was one of the longest sections. But then next to that is the issue of anxiety and worry over the things of this life, which is often connected with money and things.

Look at Matthew 6:25: "'Therefore I say to you, do not worry about your life, what you will eat or what you will drink; nor about your body, what you will put on. Is not life more than food and the body more than clothing?'" What was Jesus talking about here? I mean, food is pretty important, and clothes for most of us are a necessity, but those things are not your whole life. Life is more than the material things of this world. It is the internal and eternal things that matter. And those should be our focus. How do I know that? Well, He told us in Matthew 6:33, "'But seek first the kingdom of God and His righteousness, and all these things shall be added to you.'"

Notice the comparison here to the birds and the flowers, which show that provision is not by some kind of miraculous intervention, although that can and does occur. It is through the divine structure of creation. Birds do what they do, and God's design is to provide for them because they're doing what they're supposed to do. If we do what we're created to do, we'll have what we need. That means we are to use our ability to serve God, but our focus should not be on acquiring the things of this life. Matthew 6:19 says, "'Do not lay up for yourselves treasures on earth, where moth and rust destroy and where thieves break in and steal.'" Storing up riches and wealth and things on this earth will never satisfy us.

John D. Rockefeller, one of the wealthiest men ever to live in this country, responded to the question, How much money does it take to make a man happy? His response was, "Just one more dollar." It's never enough. Look at Matthew 6:34: "'Therefore do not worry about tomorrow, for tomorrow will worry about its own things. Sufficient for the day is its own trouble.'" Do not be anxious about tomorrow. Rather, take the appropriate action today.

Look at what Paul wrote to the Philippians regarding this topic: "Be anxious for nothing, but in everything by prayer and supplication, with thanksgiving, let your requests be made known to God" (4:6). Don't be anxious. Pray with a heart of thanksgiving, giving gratitude for God even in the challenging circumstances. I know that can be difficult, but as we go to God with thanksgiving, we know He's going to respond and He's going to see us through. Look what happens in Philippians 4:7: "And the peace of God, which surpasses all understanding, will guard your hearts and minds through Christ Jesus."

With Matthew 7, we conclude the longest discourse of Jesus in the Bible. Let's look at verse 1: "'Judge not, that you be not judged.'" As you know, this verse is taken out of context and misquoted more than it's properly used. Is Jesus saying here that we should make no moral judgments about others and about the world in which we live? If He is, then what do we do with verse 6: "'Do not give what is holy to the dogs; nor cast your pearls before swine, lest they trample them under their feet, and turn and tear you in pieces'"? He's not talking about dogs and pigs. He's talking about people. He is talking about making moral distinctions.

Then look at verses 15–16: "'Beware of false prophets, who come to you in sheep's clothing, but inwardly they are ravenous wolves. You will know them by their fruits. Do men gather grapes from thornbushes or figs from thistles?'" Obviously, we must judge between harmless animals (sheep) and dangerous ones (wolves), between good and bad fruit, then act upon that knowledge. How do you do that unless you judge? This often-misused passage on judgment is about the standard that we use and the motive for the judgment. Quoting from the Jamieson, Fausset, and Brown commentary on the Bible, "The thing here condemned is that disposition to look unfavorably on the character and actions of others, which leads invariably to the pronouncing of rash, unjust, and unlovely judgments upon them."[3] It is not the judgment here that is condemned but the hypocritical and unloving spirit from which the judgment comes. That's what Jesus is talking about.

Let's continue in Matthew 7:2, "'For with what judgment you judge, you will be judged; and with the measure you use, it will be measured back to you.'" Whose standard are you using, and are you measuring yourself by the same standard? That's what Jesus said. Now how do we arrive at the right judgment? How do we have discernment about casting pearls before the swine? How do we make moral determinations between good and bad fruit? Look at verses 7–8: "'Ask, and it will be given to you; seek, and you will find; knock, and it will be opened to you. For everyone who asks receives, and he who seeks finds, and to him who knocks it will be opened.'" The answer is to pray. We ask God. You have most likely heard sermons and teachings from the different passages of these three chapters that are known collectively as the Sermon on the Mount. And while these teachings can stand alone, they're fully understood within the context of the entire message.

In verse 12, we have what is often referred to as the Golden Rule: "'Therefore, whatever you want men to do to you, do also to them, for this is the Law and the Prophets.'" It's a nice pocket guide or reminder of God's kingdom, but it is not the totality of it. There are some who want to make their religion based upon the

Golden Rule. That's insufficient. It only speaks to our horizontal relationships with our fellow humans, but it doesn't speak to our vertical relationship with God, from which human relationships flow. That's only one side. There is more to the Golden Rule.

Now the remainder of the chapter is what I describe as the altar call. Jesus has laid out the principles of the Kingdom, one that is governed from within, and it's evidenced externally in our actions. Then we have the application of this truth. What are you going to do with it? What will you do with it now that you've heard it? How will you respond? And Jesus makes it clear. There are only two choices. In the conclusion, Jesus speaks of two ways, two trees, two professions, and two builders.

Look at Matthew 7:13–14: "'Enter by the narrow gate; for wide is the gate and broad is the way that leads to destruction, and there are many who go in by it. Because narrow is the gate and difficult is the way which leads to life, and there are few who find it.'" The narrow gate to life is difficult because it is a decision to leave behind the desires and the wants of our fallen nature then to choose the way of Jesus. And that doesn't come naturally. As the Sermon on the Mount makes abundantly clear, the kingdom of God is counterintuitive. It is counter to the culture of this day. Now you might be able to find some who give lip service to what we just talked about, the Golden Rule, but in reality, it is the gold that rules today. Responding to Jesus's call to enter the Kingdom does not come easily. Listen to what Jesus said over in Luke 9:23–24: "Then He said to them all, 'If anyone desires to come after Me, let him deny himself, and take up his cross daily, and follow Me. For whoever desires to save his life will lose it, but whoever loses his life for My sake will save it.'" That is the call of the Kingdom. That is the narrow gate, the entrance to the Kingdom.

Questions for Reflection and Discussion

1. What are the elements of prayer according to Jesus (see 6:9–13)?
   a. Honoring God's name
   b. Seeking God's kingdom and will
   c. Asking for daily needs
   d. Pleading for forgiveness
   e. Avoiding temptation
   f. All of the above

2. What is the "Golden Rule" according to Jesus (see 7:12)?

Notes on Today's Bible Reading

— Day 5 —

Reflection on Matthew 1–7

Sunday Reflection and Discussion

Gather with family or friends and use the guide below for a time of prayer, reflection, and discussion:

- Opening Prayer – Praise and a brief prayer for spiritual insight and unity.
- Recap – Briefly summarize Matthew 1–7.
- Discussion Questions – Use open-ended, age-appropriate prompts to spark meaningful worldview conversations. Here are some suggestions:
    1. Most meaningful passage that spoke to you personally?
    2. Insights gained about God: Who He is, What He values and expects, How He works?
    3. Applications that we can make from the Word to what is happening in the world?
    4. How would God have you apply His truth to your life personally?
- Action Steps – Encourage each family member to share a personal takeaway or action step for living the truth revealed in God's Word.
- Closing Prayer – Conclude by praising God for how He has revealed Himself, His purposes, and His ways, and by

praying for His help in living in the light of His truth and sharing it with others during the week ahead.

Additional Notes

— Day 6 —

Today's Reading: Matthew 8–9

Verse of the Day

> And when He had come into the house, the blind men came to Him. And Jesus said to them, "Do you believe that I am able to do this?" They said to Him, "Yes, Lord."
>
> — *Matthew 9:28*

Please read the entire Scripture selection in your own Bible and highlight or underline verses that stand out to you before you read the observations and engage the questions below.

Matthew 9:28 is our key verse from a passage about one of the many miracles Jesus performed. Have you ever considered the question what are miracles made of? Matthew 8 and 9 record ten specific miracles. It is not a chronological nor a comprehensive listing of all the miracles of Jesus (see 8:16 and 9:35). I think the two chapters provide a sampling representative, as each miracle recorded in Matthew reveals a different set of circumstances.

The first two miracles we read of are in Matthew 8:2–8:

> And behold, a leper came and worshiped Him, saying, "Lord, if You are willing, You can make me clean." Then Jesus put out His hand and touched him, saying, "I am willing; be

> cleansed." Immediately his leprosy was cleansed. And Jesus said to him, "See that you tell no one; but go your way, show yourself to the priest, and offer the gift that Moses commanded, as a testimony to them." Now when Jesus had entered Capernaum, a centurion came to Him, pleading with Him, saying, "Lord, my servant is lying at home paralyzed, dreadfully tormented." And Jesus said to him, "I will come and heal him." The centurion answered and said, "Lord, I am not worthy that You should come under my roof. But only speak a word, and my servant will be healed."

The third miracle concerns Peter's mother-in-law. Look at 8:14–15: "Now when Jesus had come into Peter's house, He saw his wife's mother lying sick with a fever. So He touched her hand, and the fever left her. And she arose and served them." Interestingly, the Gospel of Luke (a doctor) provides a little more information about this miracle: "Now He arose from the synagogue and entered Simon's house. But Simon's wife's mother was sick with a high fever, and they made request of Him concerning her" (Luke 4:38). Now we assume "they" is referring to the family who asked Jesus to heal her. Following the healing of Peter's mother-in-law, we read this in Matthew 8:16: "When evening had come, they brought to Him many who were demon-possessed. And He cast out the spirits with a word, and healed all who were sick." We don't have the specifics on each one of those cases, but it's one of the verses telling us Jesus healed and delivered many more people.

The fourth specific miracle we see recorded here by Matthew is in verse 26. This was when the disciples were in a boat. Matthew 8:24–25 says, "And suddenly a great tempest arose on the sea, so that the boat was covered with the waves. But He was asleep. Then

His disciples came to Him and awoke Him, saying, 'Lord, save us! We are perishing!'" Here we see the disciples cried out in fear and desperation as they were in a storm. (I guess it was being driven by climate change; I don't know.)

The fifth specific miracle is in regard to demonic activity. It begins in Matthew 8:28. Now when we read this, it appears there is more than one demon. This is Matthew's account, and Mark's and Luke's Gospels make reference to just one, so it might be a different occurrence. We don't know for sure, but in either case, these individuals were not in a position to ask for help. In fact, it's the opposite. Let's look at Matthew 8:28–29: "When He had come to the other side, to the country of the Gergesenes, there met Him two demon-possessed men, coming out of the tombs, exceedingly fierce, so that no one could pass that way. And suddenly they cried out, saying, 'What have we to do with You, Jesus, You Son of God? Have You come here to torment us before the time?'"

Just a note there, these demons knew Jesus. And it's interesting that they knew a lot—they had a long understanding of history and also the future. Now let me jump to where Mark records demonic activity in Mark 5:7: "And he cried out with a loud voice and said, 'What have I to do with You, Jesus, Son of the Most High God? I implore You by God that You do not torment me.'" Again, this was the demon speaking as we see Jesus interacted with the power controlling the man. Jesus delivered him, then we read that he was clothed and in his right mind in Luke's account. Also, Mark includes the fact that the man asked to go with Jesus when He was departing in the boat.

The sixth specific miracle we see in these two chapters is about a paralytic in Matthew 9:2: "Then behold, they brought to Him a paralytic lying on a bed. When Jesus saw their faith, He said to the paralytic, 'Son, be of good cheer; your sins are forgiven you.'" Luke includes more of this miracle and the faith that Jesus saw and made reference to: "Then behold, men brought on a bed a man who was paralyzed, whom they sought to bring in and lay before Him. And when they could not find how they might bring him in, because of the crowd, they went up on the housetop and let him down with his bed through the tiling into the midst before Jesus. When He saw their faith, He said to him, 'Man, your sins are forgiven you'" (Luke 5:18–20).

Look what it says there: "When He saw their faith." This sentence is worthy of study, but in this case, I want to include only a comment. You might say, "I thought faith was the substance of things hoped for, the evidence of things not seen," as we read over in Hebrews. Yes, but the faith that is unseen in the heart, if real, will manifest itself in our actions. And that was the case here, where these friends of this man were determined to bring him to Jesus. They had faith that Jesus could heal him, but they knew they had to get the man to Jesus. Their faith prompted action. The line was too long and the crowd too large, but instead of giving up and going home, they went onto the roof and lowered the man through a hole into the presence of Jesus. Those are the type of friends you want—the ones who will not give up in getting you to Jesus. And that's also the type of friend we should be.

The seventh miracle is the daughter of a ruler. Look at Matthew 9:18: "While He spoke these things to them, behold, a ruler came and worshiped Him, saying, 'My daughter has just died, but come and lay Your hand on her and she will live.'" The eighth miracle is the woman with the issue of blood in verse 21: "For she said to herself, 'If only I may touch His garment, I shall be made well.'" The ninth is the miracle of the blind men receiving sight in verses 27–28: "When Jesus departed from there, two blind men followed Him, crying out and saying, 'Son of David, have mercy on us!' And when He had come into the house, the blind men came to Him. And Jesus said to them, 'Do you believe that I am able to do this?' They said to Him, 'Yes, Lord.'" Finally, the tenth miracle is the mute man. Look at verse 32, "As they went out, behold, they brought to Him a man, mute and demon-possessed," and he was healed.

Let's summarize the miracles based upon what we have in chapters 8–9 of Matthew's Gospel. In this account, several asked for healing. Those were the leper and the blind men. One reached out without saying a word. That was the woman with the issue of blood. Two sought Jesus on behalf of others, the centurion and the ruler. And there were three occasions where friends brought those in need to Jesus, in the case of the paralytic and the mute man, or brought Jesus to them, in the case of Peter's mother-in-law. On one occasion, Jesus saw the need and He met it. That was the demonized man in the graveyard. And on one occasion, the disciples cried out collectively for help as their boat appeared to be sinking. Three of these miracles that we just read of specifically mentioned demons and demonic activity.

So, what did these ten miracles have in common? Number 1 was the presence of a need and an acknowledgment of that need in most cases. I think that the demonized man was beyond being able to recognize his need, and the Lord had mercy on him. But for the rest of them, there was the presence of a need, then number 2 was the presence of faith to have that need filled. And number 3 was the presence of the person of Jesus. He was the one who met the need, and it was the faith placed in Him. Jesus makes all the difference!

Questions for Reflection and Discussion

1. How did the centurion impress Jesus, and what eye-opening response did Jesus give about Gentiles who believe and the Jews who do not (see Matt. 8:5–13)?

2. When Jesus looked out at the crowds, what was His response (see 9:35–38)?
   a. Viewed them with compassion because of their condition
   b. Voiced the need for prayer for harvesters among them
   c. Both of the above
   d. Neither of the above

Notes on Today's Bible Reading

— Day 7 —

Today's Reading: Matthew 10–11

Verse of the Day

> "He who finds his life will lose it, and he who loses his life for My sake will find it."
>
> — *Matthew 10:39*

Please read the entire Scripture selection in your own Bible and highlight or underline verses that stand out to you before you read the observations and engage the questions below.

Today our journey brings us to Matthew 10 and 11. Our key verse is 10:39: "'He who finds his life will lose it, and he who loses his life for My sake will find it.'" Now Jesus was moving into the practical application of the paradoxical realities of the kingdom of God. Do you want to find your life? Lose it. Do you want to be a conqueror? Surrender to Jesus. Want the abundant life? Die to yourself and you'll find it. There is a lot more in these two chapters than I will comment on here. In fact, I'm going to focus primarily on chapter 10, but please be sure and read both chapters in their entirety—some good principles for Kingdom living are in them.

First look at Matthew 10:1: "And when He had called His twelve disciples to Him, He gave them power over unclean spirits, to cast them out, and to heal all kinds of sickness and all kinds of disease." Jesus called his twelve disciples, who were about to become the twelve apostles, and He gave them both power and authority, which actually Luke makes clear in his account (see 9:1). If you have the power but not the authority, you're a renegade or an outlaw. If you have the authority but no power, it quite likely is not going to end well. We need both the power and the authority from God to accomplish the mission He has given us.

Matthew then included a listing of the twelve disciples, and Jesus gave them direction for their specific mission. Let's look at 10:5–6: "These twelve Jesus sent out and commanded them, saying: 'Do not go into the way of the Gentiles, and do not enter a city of the Samaritans. But go rather to the lost sheep of the house of Israel.'" Their mission before the cross was to the Jewish nation. Contrast Jesus's instructions here to the instructions He gave post-crucifixion and resurrection, which we read over in Acts 1:8: "'But you shall receive power when the Holy Spirit has come upon you; and you shall be witnesses to Me in Jerusalem, and in all Judea and Samaria, and to the end of the earth.'"

Let's go back to Matthew and look at 10:7–11: "And as you go, preach, saying, 'The kingdom of heaven is at hand.' Heal the sick, cleanse the lepers, raise the dead, cast out demons. Freely you have received, freely give. Provide neither gold nor silver nor copper in your money belts, nor bag for your journey, nor two tunics, nor sandals, nor staffs; for a worker is worthy of his food. 'Now whatever city or town you enter, inquire who in it is worthy, and stay there till you go out.'"

Drop down to Matthew 10:14–15: "And whoever will not receive you nor hear your words, when you depart from that house or city, shake off the dust from your feet. Assuredly, I say to you, it will be more tolerable for the land of Sodom and Gomorrah in the day of judgment than for that city!" Notice something here as we go through the NT. We've seen this in the OT, too, but Sodom and Gomorrah are used as a standard of sin and judgment. From here, there are warnings of the opposition the disciples would encounter and how they were to respond to it. And this has application beyond their limited mission during Jesus's three-year ministry that goes into the age of the church, which we're in today. And note what it says in verse 16: "'Behold, I send you out as sheep in the midst of wolves. Therefore be wise as serpents and harmless as doves.'" First, notice who's sending. Jesus was sending, and He also sends us. That's the Great Commission. Second, notice how to go: "Be wise as serpents and harmless as doves." We hear this a lot, but what does it mean? Well, one commentator described it as "unflinching zeal and calm discretion."[4]

Let's continue in 10:17–20: "But beware of men, for they will deliver you up to councils and scourge you in their synagogues. You will be brought before governors and kings for My sake, as a testimony to them and to the Gentiles. But when they deliver you up, do not worry about how or what you should speak. For it will be given to you in that hour what you should speak; for it is not you who speak, but the Spirit of your Father who speaks in you." This does not mean we should not know what we believe or how to defend what we believe. It means we're not to be worried or anxious about such occasions when they arise as the Holy Spirit will guide us. Look at verse 21: "Now brother will deliver up brother to death, and a father his child; and children will rise up against parents and cause them to be put to death." Now, this is unnatural. And Jesus actually expanded on it in verses 34–36. This type of division in the family reveals the intensity of the spiritual warfare taking place between the kingdom of God and the kingdom of Satan, which he has temporarily set up on this earth. And we actually see this happening in our culture today, and frankly, it's been fostered by elements of our own government.

Let's continue in Matthew 10:22: "And you will be hated by all for My name's sake. But he who endures to the end will be saved." I want you to notice something here. Jesus put the warning out quite clearly. Nothing is hidden in the small print with Jesus. There is a price associated with following Jesus. In fact, verse 38 spells it out: "And he who does not take his cross and follow after Me is not worthy of Me." We must take up our cross, which means we have to be willing to die. Notice also it says here that he who endures to the end will be saved. This is not saying that our endurance saves us, but rather our endurance is evidence of our genuine salvation. We must hold fast to what we believe because our beliefs are anchored in the truth of God, and we are sealed by the Holy Spirit.

Here's why followers of Jesus should not be surprised by the hatred and rejection we experience from those who are outside the kingdom of God and hostile to it: "'A disciple is not above his teacher, nor a servant above his master. It is enough for a disciple that he be like his teacher, and a servant like his master. If they have called the master of the house Beelzebub, how much more will they call those of his household!'" (vv. 24–25). They did it to Jesus, and they will do it to those who truly follow Him as well. Notice, however, He immediately transitioned to, "Don't be afraid." Opposition is coming. They hated Him, and in fact, it's going to intensify and they're going to see their Master crucified. But, "Therefore do not fear them. For there is nothing covered that will not be revealed, and hidden that will not be known" (v. 26). Drop down to verses 28–31: "And do not fear those who kill the body but cannot kill the soul.

But rather fear Him who is able to destroy both soul and body in hell. Are not two sparrows sold for a copper coin? And not one of them falls to the ground apart from your Father's will. But the very hairs of your head are all numbered. Do not fear therefore; you are of more value than many sparrows." You see, if we fear God, who is able to destroy both body and soul, we won't have fear of man.

And look what it says to those who do not shrink back but faithfully endure: "'Therefore whoever confesses Me before men, him I will also confess before My Father who is in heaven. But whoever denies Me before men, him I will also deny before My Father who is in heaven'" (vv. 32–33). Now you might be saying, "Wait, there's just too much conflict here. I thought Jesus was all about peace." Look at Matthew 10:34–39:

> "Do not think that I came to bring peace on earth. I did not come to bring peace but a sword. For I have come to 'set a man against his father, a daughter against her mother, and a daughter-in-law against her mother-in-law'; and 'a man's enemies will be those of his own household.' He who loves father or mother more than Me is not worthy of Me. And he who loves son or daughter more than Me is not worthy of Me. And he who does not take his cross and follow after Me is not worthy of Me. He who finds his life will lose it, and he who loses his life for My sake will find it."

As counterintuitive as it is, we have to choose to follow God. And when we follow Him, we will see the epic spiritual warfare that is raging. The two kingdoms, the kingdom of light and the kingdom of darkness, are incompatible. Jesus is leading the kingdom of light. He is building it in the hearts of men, women, and children today.

The kingdom of darkness, which is grasping for power and to hold on, knowing what is coming, expresses that hatred toward those who are in the kingdom of light.

And here's something that will really send the Left bonkers: peace comes through conquest not compromise and capitulation. That said, however, our conquest is spiritual. It's not physical. Jesus Himself will accomplish both spiritual and physical conquest when He returns the second time. Now lest you're overwhelmed by what Jesus is calling you to, let me jump to the last three verses of Matthew 11: "'Come to Me, all you who labor and are heavy laden, and I will give you rest. Take My yoke upon you and learn from Me, for I am gentle and lowly in heart, and you will find rest for your souls. For My yoke is easy and My burden is light'" (vv. 28–30). You see, Jesus offers internal peace in the midst of external tribulation. He said it over in John 16:33, "'These things I have spoken to you, that in Me you may have peace. In the world you will have tribulation; but be of good cheer, I have overcome the world.'"

Questions for Reflection and Discussion

1. How did Jesus equip those whom He sent out (see Matthew 10)?

2. What did Jesus say to those who are burdened, like an ox pulling an overloaded cart (see 11:28–30)?
   a. Come to Him with your burdens, and He will give you rest.
   b. Take His yoke (submit to Him and His rules for life) and learn from Him.
   c. With Him in the yoke with you, His way is easy and His burden is light.
   d. All of the above.

Notes on Today's Bible Reading

— Day 8 —

Today's Reading: Matthew 12

Verse of the Day

> "A good man out of the good treasure of his heart brings forth good things, and an evil man out of the evil treasure brings forth evil things."
>
> — *Matthew 12:35*

Please read the entire Scripture selection in your own Bible and highlight or underline verses that stand out to you before you read the observations and engage the questions below.

Today we are studying Matthew 12. There's a lot in this chapter. Probably close to a dozen individual studies or sermons could be taught or preached from this one chapter alone. So I encourage you to read the entire chapter. As I've said before, it's helpful to take some notes. The Holy Spirit may just draw you to a particular verse or passage that you may want to jot down. You might want to take a deeper look into it by using a Bible commentary. Matthew Henry's commentary on the whole Bible is one that I recommend. But make sure you're reading these entire passages. I can only scratch the surface in this brief devotional commentary.

I've entitled this study "What Do Your Words Reveal?" I'm going to focus on verses 34–37, but I want to remind you how important context is. As you've gone through this journey, no doubt you've read familiar passages and verses or you've heard sermons about specific ones. But to have true application of the Word of God, we must look at them in context. It's a key principle of interpretation of Scripture. First, we need to look at them in context. We also want to see that it is consistent with Scripture elsewhere. Scripture uses Scripture to interpret Scripture. So I encourage you to read the entire passage so that you see it in context and you see the whole picture unfolding through God's Word.

Matthew 12:1–21 contains three main sections: (1) Jesus's teachings about the Sabbath (vv. 1–8), (2) His healing of a man with a withered hand (vv. 9–14), and (3) a prophecy about His servant (vv. 15–21). In verses 1–8, Jesus and His disciples were walking through grainfields on the Sabbath, and the disciples began to pick heads of grain and eat them. However, the Pharisees accused them of breaking the Sabbath law. Jesus responded by referring to David eating the consecrated bread and the priests working on the Sabbath. He emphasized that mercy is more important than sacrifice and declared Himself as the Lord of the Sabbath. The point is that the Sabbath is meant for God's worship as well as our rest and renewal, which is far more important than rigidly following man-made rules.

In verses 9–14, Jesus entered a synagogue where there was a man with a withered hand. Yet the Pharisees asked Jesus if it was lawful to heal on the Sabbath, hoping to accuse Him. Then Jesus responded by asking if they would rescue a sheep that fell into a pit on the Sabbath. He then healed the man, demonstrating that it was lawful to do good on the Sabbath. The result is that the Pharisees began to plot to kill Jesus. The point is that showing compassion and helping others should not be limited by time or day. So we should challenge legalism and focus on the spirit of God's law.

In verses 15–21, Jesus was fully aware of the Pharisees' plot, and He withdrew, but many followed Him. He healed all the sick among them but warned them not to tell others about Him. This fulfilled the prophecy of Isaiah about God's chosen Servant, who would bring justice to the nations and hope to the Gentiles (see Isa. 42:1–4), which is the longest OT quotation in Matthew's Gospel. The point here is that Jesus was the long-awaited fulfillment of the promise of the Messiah.

Next let's look at Matthew 12:22–24:

"Then one was brought to Him who was demon-possessed, blind and mute; and He healed him, so that the blind and mute man both spoke and saw. And all the multitudes were amazed and said, 'Could this be the Son of David?' Now when the Pharisees heard it they said, 'This fellow does not cast out demons except by Beelzebub, the ruler of the demons.'" Interestingly, the crowds thought Jesus was the Messiah, the greater Son of David. Yet the Pharisees claimed He was demon possessed. Now we just read that Jesus warned His disciples they were going to be saying things about them. In fact, He basically said, "If they called Me the ruler of the house Beelzebub, what are they going to say about you?" And this is true today for those who live for and follow Jesus Christ and live out the Word of God. In many cases, there are some in the world who call us haters because we uphold the truth of God so that others might come to know Jesus and the abundant life that He has. So, we shouldn't be surprised by that. We see here, Jesus Himself is called the ruler of demons.

Let's continue in Matthew 12:25–26: "But Jesus knew their thoughts, and said to them: 'Every kingdom divided against itself is brought to desolation, and every city or house divided against itself will not stand. If Satan casts out Satan, he is divided against himself. How then will his kingdom stand?" Interestingly, Abraham Lincoln based one of his more famous speeches on this very passage, referring to the antislavery north in conflict with the proslavery south: "'A house divided against itself cannot stand.' I believe this government cannot endure, permanently half slave and half free. I do not expect the Union to be dissolved—I do not expect the house to fall—but I do expect it will cease to be divided. It will become all one thing, or all the other."[5]

Jesus continues in verses 27–30:

> "'And if I cast out demons by Beelzebub, by whom do your sons cast them out? Therefore they shall be your judges. But if I cast out demons by the Spirit of God, surely the kingdom of God has come upon you. Or how can one enter a strong man's house and plunder his goods, unless he first binds the strong man? And then he will plunder his house. He who is not with Me is against Me, and he who does not gather with Me scatters abroad.'"

Now, that's a clear statement. Either you are for God or you're not. There's no gray area in the kingdom of God. Again: "He who is not with Me is against Me, and he who does not gather with Me scatters abroad.'" There's no median in the Kingdom, no middle ground. Either you're for the Lord Jesus or you're against Him.

Let's continue in Matthew 12:31–32, "'Therefore I say to you, every sin and blasphemy will be forgiven men, but the blasphemy against the Spirit will not be forgiven men. Anyone who speaks a word against the Son of Man, it will be forgiven him; but whoever speaks against the Holy Spirit, it will not be forgiven him, either in this age or in the age to come.'" This is referred to as the unpardonable sin. Admittedly, this is a study in and of itself, but the Pharisees and the Sadducees were getting perilously close to committing this sin. Here's the bottom line: The unpardonable sin is the continued rejection of Jesus Christ to whom the Holy Spirit bears witness.

OK, so how is rejecting Jesus equal to blasphemy against the Spirit? These religious leaders were watching the work of the Holy Spirit in the life and ministry of Jesus and labeling it as demonic. There is no other way to look at what they were doing except committing blasphemy. When a person continues to reject the testimony of the Holy Spirit about Jesus, ignoring the Spirit's ministry to convict us of sin, righteousness, and the judgment (see John 16:8–15), and that person dies a sinner, that is the point of no return. When your life is over and you enter eternity, there's no turning back, no changing it. So in that sense, it is the unpardonable sin. We've been given the opportunity in this life to accept the redemptive work of the Holy Spirit and surrender to Christ, but we continued to reject Him until we die. Again, that's a much deeper study.

Let's continue in Matthew 12:33–37:

> "Either make the tree good and its fruit good, or else make the tree bad and its fruit bad; for a tree is known by its fruit. Brood of vipers! How can you, being evil, speak good things? For out of the abundance of the heart the mouth speaks. A good man out of the good treasure of his heart brings forth good things, and an evil man out of the evil treasure brings forth evil things. But I say to you that for every idle word men may speak, they will give account of it

> in the day of judgment. For by your words you will be justified, and by your words you will be condemned."

In these last few verses, I want to focus on the revealing nature of our words. Jesus said our words reveal our heart. Proverbs 27:19 says, "As in water face reflects face, so a man's heart reveals the man."

The question is, "What do your words reveal about you?" You probably recall that the bank Capital One has this question in an advertisement: "What's in your wallet?" Well, I want to ask, "What's in your heart?" We must not try to excuse our idle words because Jesus says they will not be excused. Rather, we will give an account for those words. Now, as for those who have trusted Christ, as Romans 10:9–10 says, "That if you confess with your mouth the Lord Jesus and believe in your heart that God has raised Him from the dead, you will be saved. For with the heart one believes unto righteousness, and with the mouth confession is made unto salvation." So when we're talking about giving an account, we're not talking about losing our salvation. But we are talking about the fact that we will all give an account for what we do with our lives. And if we have confessed Jesus Christ and believe in our hearts, we will be saved. But we will give an account for those words that we speak.

Saved people are not perfect people. I continue to say things I think I should not have said. We repent of that and we are forgiven of that. We're not perfect, but we are and should be undergoing the process of sanctification, meaning we're moving in the right direction. The sanctification process comes about by the work of the Holy Spirit in our lives and the Word of God. We're sanctified as we read the Word of God and the Lord speaks to us and the Holy Spirit works in us. We're being sanctified.

Consequently, the words that we speak are reflective of what is happening inside of us in our hearts. So as believers, as followers of Jesus Christ, our words should be reflective of the regeneration, of the sanctification that's taking place in our lives as we spend time in prayer and as we spend time in the Word of God. Thank God I'm not what I was yesterday or last year, but also thank God I'm not what I'm going to be tomorrow, hopefully and prayerfully, as I seek the Lord and as I walk with Him. So what do your words reveal? It's a good test to see where we are in our walk with the Lord.

Questions for Reflection and Discussion

1. What did Jesus say His relationship was to the Sabbath (see vv. 1–8)?

2. According to Jesus, how does a person commit the "unpardonable sin" (see vv. 22–32)?
   a. Talk bad about Jesus personally
   b. Condemn the work of the Holy Spirit, which is mainly to point to Jesus as satanic, thus rejecting Him
   c. Blaspheme religious leaders
   d. None of the above

Notes on Today's Bible Reading

— Day 9 —

Today's Reading: Matthew 13

Verse of the Day

> "Again, the kingdom of heaven is like treasure hidden in a field, which a man found and hid; and for joy over it he goes and sells all that he has and buys that field."
>
> —*Matthew 13:44*

Please read the entire Scripture selection in your own Bible and highlight or underline verses that stand out to you before you read the observations and engage the questions below.

Today we move into the middle portion of Matthew with chapter 13. We're going to be reading the parables of Jesus. His open message about the kingdom was met with hostility and rejection, so then He began to communicate with parables.

Let's start with the definition of a parable. It is a short story—usually an illustration of a common activity, but it reveals a divine spiritual truth. Often the human mind thinks in pictures when processing. Like when someone's talking to you or you're reading a book. That's why reading is so powerful; you're creating images in your mind. So parables are powerful.

This kind of reminds me of when I was a kid. We'd go into the doctor's office or dentist's office, and they had *Highlight* magazines. Toward the back of the magazine was an illustration that included hidden objects, and you had to find those objects. Parables are kind of like that. Deep, profound spiritual truths are hidden in these stories, but they can only be found by the open eye and attentive ear. And of course, the Scripture says in Matthew 7:7, "Seek, and you will find." So if we're looking, we'll find them. But if our minds are closed, we'll miss them.

Jesus spoke somewhere in the neighborhood of thirty parables. Some scholars put the number a little higher, some lower. Some count the analogies He uses as parables; some do not. For instance, in chapter 13 there are seven parables. Some say there are eight because they count verse 52 as a parable as well, but some say it's merely an analogy.

The first parable of the sower and the seed actually introduces all seven parables and sets the discourse of Jesus in this chapter. Let's start by looking at this parable in verses 3–9:

> Then He spoke many things to them in parables, saying: "Behold, a sower went out to sow. And as he sowed, some seed fell by the wayside; and the birds came and devoured them. Some fell on stony places, where they did not have much earth; and they immediately sprang up because they had no depth of earth. But when the sun was up they were scorched, and because they had no root they withered away. And some fell among thorns, and the thorns sprang up and choked them. But others fell on good ground and yielded a crop: some a hundredfold, some sixty, some thirty. He who has ears to hear, let him hear!"

After telling this parable, His disciples came and asked for further clarification. So beginning in verse 18, Jesus provided the explanation of this parable:

> "Therefore hear the parable of the sower: When anyone hears the word of the kingdom, and does not understand it, then the wicked one comes and snatches away what was sown in his heart. This is he who received seed by the wayside. But he who received the seed on stony places, this is he who hears the word and immediately receives it with joy; yet he has no root in himself, but endures only for a while. For when tribulation or persecution arises because of the word, immediately he stumbles. Now he who received seed among the thorns is he who hears the word, and the cares of this world and the deceitfulness of riches choke the word, and he becomes unfruitful. But he who received seed on the good ground is he who hears the word and understands it, who indeed bears fruit and produces: some a hundredfold, some sixty, some thirty." (vv. 18–23)

Now this parable gives us some direction on how to pray as the gospel message goes forth into the hearts of people. I often pray along the following lines when I'm preaching: Pray for (1) Understanding so that this word that is implanted, the truth of God, will be understood. (2) Courage—the courage to accept it and live it out. (3) Endurance to be able to go the distance with this truth and not fall away halfway through. We want to finish strong as followers of Jesus Christ. And (4) come to maturity and bear fruit—much fruit. Those are really the four ways to pray about the message of the gospel, the truth of the Word of God going forth.

What follows are six more parables that are actually paired. So in the rest of the chapter, there are three pairs of parables. The second parable of the wheat and the tares or the weeds, which is the one that I want to look at in greater detail, corresponds to the seventh parable in this chapter, the parable of the dragnet. The third and fourth parables speak to the growth of the kingdom of God, and the fifth and sixth parables speak to the priceless value of the kingdom of God, the truth of God.

Let's move now to the parable of the wheat and the tares in Matthew 13:24–30:

> Another parable He put forth to them, saying: "The kingdom of heaven is like a man who sowed good seed in his field; but while men slept, his enemy came and sowed tares among the wheat and went his way. But when the grain had sprouted and produced a crop, then the tares also appeared. So the servants of the owner came and said to him, "Sir, did you not sow good seed in your field? How then does it have tares?" He said to them, "An enemy has done this." The servants said to him, "Do you want us then to go and gather them up?" But he said, "No, lest while you gather up the tares you also uproot the wheat with them. Let both grow together until the harvest, and at the time of harvest I will say to the reapers, 'First gather together the tares and bind them in bundles to burn them, but gather the wheat into my barn.'"

Then skip to verses 34–43:

> All these things Jesus spoke to the multitude in parables; and without a parable He did not speak to them, that it might be fulfilled which was spoken by the prophet, saying:
>
> "I will open My mouth in parables;
> I will utter things kept secret from the foundation of the world."
>
> Then Jesus sent the multitude away and went into the house. And His disciples came to Him, saying, "Explain to us the parable of the tares of the field." He answered and said to them: "He who sows the good seed is the Son of Man. The field is the world, the good seeds are the sons of the kingdom, but the tares are the sons of the wicked one. The enemy who sowed them is the devil, the harvest is the end of the age, and the reapers are the angels. Therefore as the tares are gathered and burned in the fire, so it will be at the end of this age. The Son of Man will send out His angels, and they will gather out of His kingdom all things that offend, and those who practice lawlessness, and will cast them into the furnace of fire. There will be wailing and gnashing of teeth. Then the righteous will shine forth as the sun in the kingdom of their Father. He who has ears to hear, let him hear!"

That is still to come, but this is an encouraging and reassuring parable. I often refer to it when I'm speaking to groups. People say, "Tony, what encourages you?" We see this unfolding right now. I think this is one of the most important parables that Jesus told that explains where we are in our culture. I think we're living right in the middle of this parable. Just a few points for your consideration here.

1. *The Reality.* There is evil in this world. Most people think that the weed referenced here is the darnel, which is poisonous to both humans and animals. The problem is that a darnel weed is almost indistinguishable from a blade of wheat in the early stages. However, as this weed grows, it becomes more pronounced and one can tell the difference. The picture here is that the enemy, Satan, has sown evil in the hearts of men, and it is manifesting and becoming more pronounced with each passing day. But notice, so is the good.

2. *The Responsibility.* Jesus gives us our responsibility here in this parable and it's not to uproot the evil. While it is not explicitly stated, I assume it's understood that our responsibility is to simply tend the wheat. Don't focus on the weeds. Do we need to know what's there and have awareness? Absolutely. But focus on tending the wheat. Scripture tells us not to think on evil things but to think on good things—those that bring glory to God, which build us up.

3. *The Result.* Jesus makes clear that the harvest is coming, the great separation where the weeds will be destroyed, burned. That is a picture of hell. Yes, there is a literal hell. And the wheat will be taken into the barn, which is heaven. Yes, we see evil in the world today and it is disheartening. It's troubling; it's concerning. But we must not miss a part of the good that God is doing in our day. We don't want to be separated from God. We don't want to miss the opportunity that we have to be a part of what God is doing in our day.

Great challenges bring great opportunities. There will be many whose hearts will turn cold toward the faith, but there will be others seeking answers, looking for hope, who will be open to the truth of the gospel. And you and I need to be prepared to share that good news. I think we are living in exciting times as we are moving closer and closer to this final harvest. Let's not get lost in the weeds. Let's stay focused on the mission that God has given us, to know Him and to make Him known. What a great parable!

Questions for Reflection and Discussion

1. What was Jesus's explanation of the parable of the wheat and weeds (vv. 36–43)?
   a. The Son of Man (Jesus) sows the good seed (sons of the Kingdom).
   b. The devil sows the bad seed (sons of the evil one).
   c. The field is the world, and the harvest is the end of the age.
   d. Reapers are angels who gather the evil for fiery torment and the good for glory.
   e. All of the above.

2. What is the main point of Jesus's twin parables of the hidden treasure and the pearl of great price (see vv. 44–46)?

Notes on Today's Bible Reading

— Day 10 —

Today's Reading: Matthew 14–15

Verse of the Day

> But Jesus said, "They do not need to go away. You give them something to eat."
>
> — *Matthew 14:16*

Please read the entire Scripture selection in your own Bible and highlight or underline verses that stand out to you before you read the observations and engage the questions below.

Today we are in Matthew 14 and 15. You've probably heard the term "power lunch." This is when business and political leaders get together and discuss plans and ideas over a meal. Then someone picks up the tab and puts it on their expense account. What we're going to look at today is what I describe as a real power lunch. Our key verse is 14:16: "But Jesus said to them, 'They do not need to go away. You give them something to eat.'"

There are so many important principles in these two chapters. As I've said before, I'm simply your tour guide pointing out some of the vistas on this journey to encourage you. I want to emphasize strongly that you need to read the passages in their entirety. What I'm providing here in this daily devotional are simply the highlights. So I'm going to give you a quick overview, and then I'm going to circle back to the miracle we call "Feeding the 5,000." It is a perfect example of what Dr. Henry Blackaby wrote about several years ago in his book *Experiencing God*, about finding out where God is working and joining Him in that work.

First, here is an overview of the two chapters. In Matthew 14:1–13, Jesus responded to the murder of John the Baptist by Herod. He went away and He prayed. Then in verses 14–23 is the feeding of the 5,000, which we will come back to as we wrap up today's study. After that, Jesus once again went away on a prayer retreat. Then in verses 24–33, Jesus walked on water and Peter needed floaties. Then we have verses 34–36 where Jesus healed all the sick who touched the hem of His garment.

In Matthew 15:1–20, Jesus turned the Pharisees' attack on His disciples based upon man-made tradition into a teaching from divine truth. In fact, I want to read a few of those verses. Look at verses 17–20: "'Do you not yet understand that whatever enters the mouth goes into the stomach and is eliminated? But those things which proceed out of the mouth come from the heart, and they defile a man. For out of the heart proceed evil thoughts, murders, adulteries, fornications, thefts, false witness, blasphemies. These are the things which defile a man, but to eat with unwashed hands does not defile a man.'"

In other words, it's what comes out of the mouth, not what goes in, that defiles a person. Then in verses 21–28, Jesus healed the daughter of a Canaanite woman, a Gentile of demon possession, because of the mother's faith, which was evidenced in large part by her persistence. Jesus told her it's not right to give the children's food to the dogs. He basically said, "I'm not going to help you," but it was a test. To her credit, she did not let it go. Jesus responded,

"Great is your faith!" Consequently, He answered her request and delivered the girl and made her whole.

Then in Matthew 15:29–39, Jesus healed the multitude, and on this occasion fed 4,000. But the disciples were still looking for takeout. They still had not connected the dots in terms of what Jesus could do.

Now let's go back to the feeding of the 5,000 in Matthew 14:13–21:

> When Jesus heard it, He departed from there by boat to a deserted place by Himself. But when the multitudes heard it, they followed Him on foot from the cities. And when Jesus went out He saw a great multitude; and He was moved with compassion for them, and healed their sick. When it was evening, His disciples came to Him, saying, "This is a deserted place, and the hour is already late. Send the multitudes away, that they may go into the villages and buy themselves food." But Jesus said to them, "They do not need to go away. You give them something to eat." And they said to Him, "We have here only five loaves and two fish." He said, "Bring them here to Me." Then He commanded the multitudes to sit down on the grass. And He took the five loaves and the two fish, and looking up to heaven, He blessed and broke and gave the loaves to the disciples; and the disciples gave to the multitudes. So, they all ate and were filled, and they took up twelve baskets full of the fragments that remained. Now those who had eaten were about five thousand men, besides women and children.

Just a note of further explanation here: There were 5,000 men, and it's not unreasonable to assume most of these men may have had a wife and possibly children, so the total number that Jesus fed on this occasion could have easily been 15,000 or many more. The disciples didn't see how they could meet the needs of so many people with their limited resources. And I think in many ways the church is still hindered by this type of thinking, especially today, as the government has crowded out the church with its apparent endless supply of money and resources. The church looks at its limited ability to minister to the needs of the people around by looking at our finite resources, rather than the infinite ability of God.

This is the only miracle account (other than the resurrection) that is recorded in all four Gospels, and I want us to read John's account because he provided a little more detail, including the origin of these five loaves. They weren't five big loaves of bread as we might find on a grocery store shelf but probably more like buns or biscuits with the two small fishes. It was a bag lunch that one lad had, probably packed by his mother as he was going with his father to the Passover feast in Jerusalem. Look with me at John 6:1–11:

> After these things Jesus went over the Sea of Galilee, which is the Sea of Tiberias. Then a great multitude followed Him, because they saw His signs which He performed on those who were diseased. And Jesus went up on the mountain, and there He sat with His disciples. Now the Passover, a feast of the Jews, was near. Then Jesus lifted up His eyes, and seeing a great multitude coming toward Him, He said to Philip, "Where shall we buy bread, that these may eat?" But this He said to test him, for He Himself knew what He would do. Philip answered Him, "Two hundred denarii

> worth of bread is not sufficient for them, that every one of them may have a little." One of His disciples, Andrew, Simon Peter's brother, said to Him, "There is a lad here who has five barley loaves and two small fish, but what are they among so many?" Then Jesus said, "Make the people sit down." Now there was much grass in the place. So the men sat down, in number about five thousand. And Jesus took the loaves, and when He had given thanks He distributed them to the disciples, and the disciples to those sitting down; and likewise of the fish, as much as they wanted.

This was probably the first time many in that crowd had been fed until they were full because people didn't have the abundance of food that we're blessed with today (by the way, a good deal of which we waste and throw out).

Yet after the meal is when John gives us some details we don't find in the other Gospels. Let's continue in John 6:12–15:

> So when they were filled, He said to His disciples, "Gather up the fragments that remain, so that nothing is lost." Therefore they gathered them up, and filled twelve baskets with the fragments of the five barley loaves which were left over by those who had eaten. Then those men, when they had seen the sign that Jesus did, said, "This is truly the Prophet who is to come into the world." Therefore when Jesus perceived that they were about to come and take Him by force to make Him king, He departed again to the mountain by Himself alone.

The “Prophet” they referred to was the One Moses predicted in Deuteronomy 18:15–18, which was a way of claiming that Jesus was the messianic “Prophet like Moses.” That is a major theme in Matthew’s Gospel with all his focus on Jesus’s activity, especially His teaching, associated with mountains. However, Jesus didn’t so much compare and contrast Himself with Moses here in John’s Gospel but rather with the manna from heaven in the time of Moses (6:22–59). He proclaimed: “I am the bread of life” (v. 35).

As we wind up our study, I’d like to focus on the boy who offered his lunch to Jesus. Now I feel pretty certain that when the boy headed out the door that morning with the lunch his mom had provided for him, he never contemplated he would be a part of a miracle of God—a miracle read about by multiplied millions of people over the years, again and again. But this is how we join God in what He is doing. We take our little insignificant contribution, and we don’t hold back, thinking of our own wants and needs. Instead, we yield what we have to Jesus. Then He gives us the opportunity to partner with Him. After all, He’s the only One who can take the bag lunch and fill the stomachs of more than 5,000 people and have twelve baskets filled with leftovers. That’s what I call a real power lunch. This little boy could have said, “If I give this up, I’m not going to have it.” But when he gave it up, it was multiplied and God used it to feed many.

Think about it for just a moment. What are you holding back? What has God given you that you’re not yielding back to Him? It’s a good question to ponder. What an amazing story here of the little boy with the five loaves and two fishes the Lord used to feed thousands of people.

Questions for Reflection and Discussion

1. What is the key lesson to learn from Peter attempting to walk on water (see 14:22–33)?
   a. Stay in the boat!
   b. Put on an approved flotation device!
   c. Keep your eyes on Jesus!
   d. None of the above.

2. What did the Canaanite mother do that proved her faith in Jesus to heal her child (see 15:21–28)?

Notes on Today's Bible Reading

— Day 11 —

Today's Reading: Matthew 16–17

Verse of the Day

> When Jesus came into the region of Caesarea Philippi, He asked His disciples, saying, "Who do men say that I, the Son of Man, am?"
>
> —*Matthew 16:13*

Please read the entire Scripture selection in your own Bible and highlight or underline verses that stand out to you before you read the observations and engage the questions below.

Our study today takes us to Matthew 16–17, and our key verse is 16:13: "When Jesus came into the region of Caesarea Philippi, He asked His disciples, saying, 'Who do men say that I, the Son of Man, am?'" In these two chapters, we see the intensifying confrontation between the religious crowd, those who were blindly looking for a sign, and Jesus, who was opening the eyes of His disciples more and more along the way about what was to come.

Sometimes Jesus had to resort to remedial education, as seen in 16:6–10: "Then Jesus said to them, 'Take heed and beware of the leaven of the Pharisees and the Sadducees.' And they reasoned among themselves, saying, 'It is because we have taken no bread.' But Jesus, being aware of it, said to them, 'O you of little faith, why do you reason among yourselves because you have brought no bread? Do you not yet understand, or remember the five loaves of the five thousand and how many baskets you took up? Nor the seven loaves of the four thousand and how many large baskets you took up?'"

So the question is, how many times do we have to see God at work to understand who He is and what He can do, even in our own lives today? Let's continue in verses 11–12: "'How is it you do not understand that I did not speak to you concerning bread?—but to beware of the leaven of the Pharisees and Sadducees.' Then they understood that He did not tell them to beware of the leaven of bread, but of the doctrine of the Pharisees and Sadducees."

Now Peter's confession regarding the identity of Jesus comes next in chapter 16, and that is where I want us to focus most of our study. But first, let's consider the content in Matthew 17, which begins with the account of the transfiguration in verses 1–8. While the transfiguration was a unique event revealing the deity of Jesus, it is a prediction of our future transformation. What happened to Christ on that mountain with Moses and Elijah is a pattern for what should progressively happen to every believer. In the transfiguration, we see not only Jesus's deity but God's original intention for humanity. Ultimately, we will be glorified. As Jesus said back in Matthew 13:43, "the righteous will shine forth as the sun in the kingdom of their Father." And Paul declared that as we follow Jesus by faith and focus in the here and now, we "are being transformed into the same image from glory to glory, just as by the Spirit of the Lord" (2 Cor. 3:18). Yet even with all of the glory on that mountain, there was the reality of the cross, which was the topic discussed by Jesus, Moses, and Elijah (see Luke 9:31). Then in Matthew 17:5 there was the affirmation of the Father: "This is My beloved Son, in whom I am well pleased." And the admonition to the disciples: "Hear Him!" What followed on their way down the mountain was yet another prediction of the cross, the necessity of Calvary. That is what the Father wanted Jesus's followers to grasp.

Then in 17:14–20, we find a fallen world and a failing church. The father of an epileptic boy represents all who come to the church desperate for help. The nine disciples at the foot of the mountain experiencing faith failure remind us of the contemporary church that doesn't have enough faith to have a positive impact. When Jesus, Peter, James, and John returned, Jesus was disappointed: "O faithless and perverse generation, how long shall I be with you? How long shall I bear with you? Bring him here to Me" (v. 17). Jesus delivered the boy of the demon, but the disciples asked why they couldn't do it. He answered in verse 20: "'Because of your unbelief; for assuredly, I say to you, if you have faith as a mustard seed, you will say to this mountain, "Move from here to there," and it will move; and nothing will be impossible for you. However, this kind does not go out except by prayer and fasting.'" The antidote to faith failure is prayer and fasting.

Now let's go back to chapter 16 and consider Peter's confession and the background for it in verses 13–15: "When Jesus came into the region of Caesarea Philippi, He asked His disciples, saying, 'Who do men say that I, the Son of Man, am?' So they said, 'Some say John the Baptist, some Elijah, and others Jeremiah or one of the prophets.' He said to them, 'But who do you say that I am?'"

That really is the big question. It's not who the world says Jesus is. It's not who the history books say that Jesus is. It's not the culture. Who do you say that He is? Let's continue in Matthew 16:16–26:

> Simon Peter answered and said, "You are the Christ, the Son of the living God." Jesus answered and said to him, 'Blessed are you, Simon Bar-Jonah, for flesh and blood has not revealed this to you, but My Father who is in heaven. And I also say to you that you are Peter, and on this rock I will build My church, and the gates of Hades shall not prevail against it. And I will give you the keys of the kingdom of heaven, and whatever you bind on earth will be bound in heaven, and whatever you loose on earth will be loosed in heaven.' Then He commanded His disciples that they should tell no one that He was Jesus the Christ. From that time Jesus began to show to His disciples that He must go to Jerusalem, and suffer many things from the elders and chief priests and scribes, and be killed, and be raised the third day. Then Peter took Him aside and began to rebuke Him, saying, "Far be it from You, Lord; this shall not happen to You!" But He turned and said to Peter, "Get behind Me, Satan! You are an offense to Me, for you are not mindful of the things of God, but the things of men." Then Jesus said to His disciples, "If anyone desires to come after Me, let him deny himself, and take up his cross, and follow Me. For whoever desires to save his life will lose it, but whoever loses his life for My sake will find it. For what profit is it to a man if he gains the whole world, and loses his own soul? Or what will a man give in exchange for his soul?'"

I want to explore three aspects of this passage: (1) the Christ, (2) the Kingdom, and (3) the Cross.

Let's start by looking at the Christ. Read 16:13 again: "When Jesus came into the region of Caesarea Philippi, He asked His disciples, saying, 'Who do men say that I, the Son of Man, am?'" First notice the location: Caesarea Philippi, which is about twenty-five miles north of Galilee. I've been there a number of times. I've actually taught there. This was a pagan city where the Greek god, Pan, was worshipped. A cave is there under a massive cliff, and pagans saw this cave as literally the gates of hell. So when Jesus was having this conversation with His disciples talking about the gates of hell, they knew exactly what He was talking about. The fertility gods entered this place and went into the underworld during the winter, then they returned in the spring. To entice the return of Pan in the spring, these pagans, these unbelievers, these Gentiles, engaged in all types of immoral behavior, sexual, immoral behavior. So Caesarea Philippi was really like a red-light district. And it was here that Jesus brought His disciples for what was basically their commencement speech after three years of being in training with Him.

Next notice the question we must ask ourselves about the Christ, and the answer cannot be what our parents said nor what our grandparents, the culture, or our pastor said. Who do you say that Jesus is? Peter answered in verse 16: "You are the Christ, the Son of the living God." Yet revelation leads to the truth. Look at how Jesus replied in verse 17: "Blessed are you, Simon Bar-Jonah, for flesh and blood has not revealed this to you, but My Father who is in heaven." Christianity is not the invention of man, but it is the invitation of God to have a relationship with Him. That's what sets Christianity apart from other religions. It's not something we created. God invited us into relationship with Him. So it is the Holy Spirit that reveals this truth to us.

First of all, some respond to the identity of Jesus with relationship, through repentance and faith. The second thing we see in this exchange about Jesus's identity is the response of religion.

Religion leads to the wrong conclusion. Look at verse 14: "So they said, 'Some say John the Baptist, some Elijah, and others Jeremiah or one of the prophets.'" Now it's not necessarily bad, but it's the wrong conclusion. And that's where religion will take us, that Jesus is just another teacher. That was where Judaism was taking them. Then there's the third category of people who respond to Jesus, and that is rebellion, just plain rebellion. It leads to a lie. Look at Matthew 12:24: "Now when the Pharisees heard it they said, 'This fellow does not cast out demons except by Beelzebub, the ruler of the demons.'" That's a flat-out lie, but that's where rebellion of the heart will lead us. The bottom line is how we answer the question about the identity of Christ and how we relate to Him.

The second aspect of this account is the Kingdom. Look at Matthew 16:18–19. "'And I also say to you that you are Peter, and on this rock I will build My church, and the gates of Hades shall not prevail against it. And I will give you the keys of the kingdom of heaven, and whatever you bind on earth will be bound in heaven, and whatever you loose on earth will be loosed in heaven.'"

Notice what Jesus said about Simon in verse 18: "And I also say to you that you are Peter, and on this rock I will build My church, and the gates of Hades shall not prevail against it." The Greek word is *petros*, which means a piece of rock—a chip off the old block, if you will. This is a play on words that Jesus was engaged in. The church is not built on Peter. That's not what Jesus was saying here. He said, "Simon, you are *petros*, a rock, a stone, but the *petra*, the bedrock, the foundation is the confession that Jesus is the Christ." That confession was the foundation upon which the church was going to be built, not Peter but Peter's confession that came from the revelation of who Jesus was, the foundation of the church. Now what's the purpose? The gates of hell shall not prevail. There's so much in this one statement that we could literally spend the entire time just here.

The gates of hell represent immorality, cultural depravity, the ideologies of this world, death. There is no fear in death. Matthew 16:25 says, "For whoever desires to save his life will lose it, but whoever loses his life for My sake will find it." This is so filled with imagery that we don't catch it; you know, we're thinking the gates of hell. Well, literally, those were the gates of hell right there to the underworld as the pagans were teaching. And Jesus said, "The gates of hell will not prevail against us." This ideology of man—this deception—will not prevail. By the way, the gates don't move. We have to charge the gates. And then there's the power and authority to do it. It's spiritual. Look at verse 19: "'And I will give you the keys of the kingdom of heaven, and whatever you bind on earth will be bound in heaven, and whatever you loose on earth will be loosed in heaven.'"

We've talked about this many, many times. The weapons of our warfare are not carnal, but they're spiritual. Notice Jesus said, "I will give." This happened at the resurrection. Jesus gave us this power in Matthew 28:18–19: "And Jesus came and spoke to them, saying, 'All authority has been given to Me in heaven and on earth. Go therefore and make disciples of all the nations.'" Remember, this is a change from what He did in His first training mission. He told them not to go beyond the boundaries of the Jewish nation. But once all authority had been given to Him because of His obedience to go to the cross, His death, burial, and resurrection—all authority—so the gates of hell cannot prevail. The ideologies of man, what we see unfolding in our culture today, this transgender nonsense, this sexual rebellion against God, the ideologies of man will not prevail if we make that profession that Jesus is Christ and we live that out.

Finally, the third aspect is the cross in Matthew 16:24: "Then Jesus said to His disciples, 'If anyone desires to come after Me, let him deny himself, and take up his cross, and follow Me.'" First, the desire. We have to pursue. We have to go after Christ. The Christian life is not passive. It's not like going through McDonald's and getting a cup of coffee or a biscuit. It's not drive through. It's not this passive thing where you just stick your hand out. It is an active pursuit. We must pursue God. Colossians 3:2 says, "Set your mind on things above, not on things on the earth." We have to be intentional about our desire to seek God. Second, we're to deny ourselves, to forget ourselves, to lose sight of our own interests, like what Jesus said here: "If you want to follow me, deny yourself." Earlier we looked at Matthew 6:33: "But seek first the kingdom of God and His righteousness, and all these things shall be added to you." And then third, here's a difficult one: "Die."

There was no other reason to take up a cross. A cross was not an ornament of affluence. It was an instrument of affliction. It was not something they wore around their necks like we do today. It was an instrument of death and persecution. The reality is, if we won't die for what we believe, it is unlikely that we will live for what we believe. So we have to be willing to lay down our lives for the truth. And that sometimes may mean only our reputation. It means maybe for relationships. It could mean any number of things, but it is dying to ourselves so that we might live for Christ. So the church's power in this hour is professing Jesus as the Christ, the Son of God, pursuing the kingdom of God in its purpose and power through picking up our own cross. The Christian walk is not passive; it is active, and the gates of hell will not prevail if we live out the Christian life as Jesus has called us to live.

Questions for Reflection and Discussion

1. What did Jesus say about Peter's confession that He was indeed the Christ, the Son of the living God (see 16:17–19)?
2. When Jesus was transfigured on the mountaintop, who appeared alongside Him (see 17:1–3)?
   a. Moses and Aaron
   b. Moses and Miriam
   c. Moses and Elijah
   d. None of the above

Notes on Today's Bible Reading

— Day 12 —

Reflection on Matthew 8–17

Sunday Reflection and Discussion

Gather with family or friends and use the guide below for a time of prayer, reflection, and discussion:

- Opening Prayer – Praise and a brief prayer for spiritual insight and unity.
- Recap – Briefly summarize Matthew 8–17.
- Discussion Questions – Use open-ended, age-appropriate prompts to spark meaningful worldview conversations. Here are some suggestions:
    1. Most meaningful passage that spoke to you personally?
    2. Insights gained about God: Who He is, What He values and expects, How He works?
    3. Applications that we can make from the Word to what is happening in the world?
    4. How would God have you apply His truth to your life personally?
- Action Steps – Encourage each family member to share a personal takeaway or action step for living the truth revealed in God's Word.
- Closing Prayer – Conclude by praising God for how He has revealed Himself, His purposes, and His ways, and by

praying for His help in living in the light of His truth and sharing it with others during the week ahead.

Additional Notes

— Day 13 —

Today's Reading: Matthew 18–19

Verse of the Day

> "But whoever causes one of these little ones who believe in Me to sin, it would be better for him if a millstone were hung around his neck, and he were drowned in the depth of the sea."
>
> — *Matthew 18:6*

Please read the entire Scripture selection in your own Bible and highlight or underline verses that stand out to you before you read the observations and engage the questions below.

Let me ask you a question as we begin today's study. Did Jesus speak to purely political issues? If you said no, you are correct because there are no purely political issues, meaning issues that belong solely to the state. What we're going to look at this morning in Matthew 18 and 19 is that Jesus spoke to issues that were spiritual at their very core, yet they were also debated in the political arena. Our key verse is Matthew 18:6: "But whoever causes one of these little ones who believe in Me to sin, it would be better for him if a millstone were hung around his neck, and he were drowned in the depth of the sea."

In these two chapters, Jesus taught on spiritual matters that have been made into political issues in our day, suggesting that somehow, because they're political, they're beyond the authority of the Scripture and of the church. Jesus spoke about children, their faith, and His concern for them. He spoke of His concern for the lost, church discipline, forgiveness, marriage, gender, wealth, and rewards in God's Kingdom. In this devotional, I want to zero in on those spiritual matters that have been or are being encroached upon by governments, that in their policies and their actions, have rejected the truth of God.

Let's start in Matthew18:1–6:

> At that time the disciples came to Jesus, saying, "Who then is greatest in the kingdom of heaven?" Then Jesus called a little child to Him, set him in the midst of them, and said, "Assuredly, I say to you, unless you are converted and become as little children, you will by no means enter the kingdom of heaven. Therefore whoever humbles himself as this little child is the greatest in the kingdom of heaven. Whoever receives one little child like this in My name receives Me. But whoever causes one of these little ones who believe in Me to sin, it would be better for him if a millstone were hung around his neck, and he were drowned in the depth of the sea."

Here Jesus told the disciples, who were jockeying for position in His kingdom, that the key is the faith and innocence of a child, just to trust and believe. That is how you enter the kingdom of heaven. But He went on, and He issued a warning to those who took advantage of the innocence and the trusting nature of children.

Just notice in this passage that all of the other crowd, the religious crowd, the leaders, were refusing to come to Jesus. They were rejecting him. But He called a child, and he came immediately to Him. That says a lot about why so many young people come to know Christ in their early years. And I'll come back to that in a moment. But Jesus said, "Do not forbid them from coming to me."

Look at this in Matthew 19:13–14: "Then little children were brought to Him that He might put His hands on them and pray, but the disciples rebuked them. But Jesus said, 'Let the little children come to Me, and do not forbid them; for of such is the kingdom of heaven.'" Now I believe Jesus inferred that the hottest place in hell is preserved for those lead children away from God or block their access to Him altogether. God's heart is clearly for the children. Jesus said, "Do not forbid them."

Let's bring this right to where we are today. How do we, in today's culture, forbid children from coming to God? Well, let's just start with what happened sixty years ago when we took prayer and the Bible out of our schools because we were told that children are very impressionable and easily influenced. And that was not the role of our schools to lead them into knowing God. Now, however, look what's happened in that vacuum that was created when God was kicked out of school. Far from teaching them that they were uniquely created by God in His image, they're now being indoctrinated, often without their parents knowledge, with things such as the twisted and perverse LGBTQ+ ideology, which corrupts and confuses children and suggests to them they can choose their own gender and they're encouraged to do whatever feels good.

This is what many teachers' unions today are advocating in the classroom, like the American Federation of Teachers. It's what the Southern Poverty Law Center is doing. Google it and find out more. It's what political administrations have been doing for years through the Department of Education. Scroll your news feed and you will see it. The Left is hiding their intentions in broad daylight. At a recent Pride Parade in New York City, they chanted, "We are queer and we're coming for your children." Now some would say, "Oh, they're just being boisterous and they're just trying to incite the other side." Well, in their pride and their arrogance, they are declaring their intentions. And it's not new—this goes back decades. In fact, the San Francisco Gay Men's Choir did something similar a few years back, singing a song that proclaimed, "We are going to convert your children." When evil speaks of the evil they plan to do to children, believe it.

If that is not convincing enough, let's revisit why children should be our focus. Like many believers, I came to know Christ as a child. I had not been in church until I was about six years old. It was at vacation Bible school. You may be acquainted with my story. Childhood is when most people come to know the Lord Jesus Christ. Children are trusting, so it is not surprising that many respond to the gospel at a young age. It has also been proven that childhood is when our worldview is formulated. The research of George Barna and others shows that a worldview is formulated between the ages of fifteen months and thirteen years. So it is critical that we invest in children.

What is a worldview? It is how we view the world around us and how we interpret the events occurring around us. This is why we saw the previous administration and the progressive left continuously wanting to get our children into government schools earlier and earlier so they can indoctrinate them. Now this social engineering is harmful and it is wrong. Parents are given the responsibility and the authority by God to train their children to love God and to follow Him. Look what Deuteronomy 6:4–7 says, "Hear, O Israel: The LORD our God, the LORD is one! You shall love the LORD your God with all your heart, with all your soul, and with all your strength. And these words which I command you today shall be in your heart. You shall teach them diligently to your children, and shall talk of them when you sit in your house, when you walk by the way, when you lie down, and when you rise up."

That's the responsibility of parents. We cannot allow the government to take our kids and indoctrinate them with something that runs 180 degrees from the truth of God's Word.

Believe it or not, here's another issue that has become political: church discipline. Look at Matthew 18:15–17: "'Moreover if your brother sins against you, go and tell him his fault between you and him alone. If he hears you, you have gained your brother. But if he will not hear, take with you one or two more, that "by the mouth of two or three witnesses every word may be established." And if he refuses to hear them, tell it to the church. But if he refuses even to hear the church, let him be to you like a heathen and a tax collector." Now I've actually had to practice this on a few occasions, and I will say, it's painful, but it works. It preserves the integrity of the church and often relationships. I still have relationships with those I've went through this with because God lays it out the way it should work in the church.

How has this been turned into a political issue? Well, maybe you've seen in recent years how a number of Catholic bishops refused the sacrament of the Eucharist to elected officials who support abortion. The Catholic Church has been abundantly clear on where it stands on the sanctity of human life. God's Word is crystal clear. However, there were congressional Democrats complaining that the Catholic Church should lose its tax exemption for "weaponizing communion." Jesus said discipline of its members was the responsibility of the church. And it's interesting, Matthew is the only Gospel that we find the word *church*, which is from the Greek word *ekklésia* and means "those who are called out." It was used in the Greek times to describe a body of citizens who gathered to discuss and act upon affairs of the state or government. So it was a community. The church was to exercise government as it considered what was happening in the broader culture to govern itself.

In Matthew 19, Jesus took on more hot-button issues: "The Pharisees also came to Him, testing Him, and saying to Him, 'Is it lawful for a man to divorce his wife for just any reason?' And He answered and said to them, 'Have you not read that He who made them at the beginning "made them male and female," and said, "For this reason a man shall leave his father and mother and be joined to his wife, and the two shall become one flesh?" So then, they are no longer two but one flesh. Therefore what God has joined together, let not man separate'" (vv. 3–6).

Here the religious crowd was trying to put Him into a box, so to speak, on marriage and divorce. They knew what God's Word taught about divorce, that God hates divorce. But if Jesus said that, He would be countering Moses and undercutting him.

For our benefit, notice where He started: with a biology lesson on gender, which frankly, our current culture could use. You might say, "Wait a minute, I thought Jesus didn't speak to these matters." Maybe not the Jesus some have made Him into, essentially in their own image—quite frankly, some have made an idol out of Jesus. That's not the Jesus who made us in His image. He spoke to these issues—even to this very issue of gender: "male and female He created them" (Gen. 1:27). Period.

Jesus then moved to marriage. Another shocker. Jesus said marriage is between a man and a woman. Yes, He said that. He also said that marriage is for life. Yes, He said that: "Therefore what God has joined together, let not man separate" (Matt. 19:6). He went on to say Moses allowed divorce because of the hardness or sinfulness of their hearts. But that's not the way God created marriage from the start.

So where does God stand on divorce? He's not in favor of it. In fact, it's interesting that Jesus then moved on to discuss children, right after He talked about divorce, because divorce affects children. In fact, divorce oftentimes alters children's understanding of their heavenly Father. But hear me, while God hates divorce (Mal. 2:16), He loves those who are divorced, those who have been hurt by divorce, those who have been a part of it. These rules are not for our restriction but are wisdom from the Creator, for our well-being. But with the Lord, what is past is past. If we confess our sins, Jesus is faithful and just to forgive us our sins and to cleanse us from all unrighteousness. No one is beyond the reach of God's grace except the person who rejects it. There is healing and there is restoration with Jesus. But we must acknowledge His Word, that it is true, and bring our lives in alignment with that truth.

Questions for Reflection and Discussion

1. What is the point of the parable of the unforgiving servant (see 18:23–35)?

2. How did Jesus reply to the question the Pharisees asked about divorce (see 19:3–9)?
    a. God made us male and female.
    b. God intends for marriage to be between one man and one woman.

c. God desires for marriage to be permanent.
d. God did not intend divorce; it is the result of the hardness of our hearts.
e. All of the above.

Notes on Today's Bible Reading

— Day 14 —

Today's Reading: Matthew 20–21

Verse of the Day

> And He said to them, "It is written, 'My house shall be called a house of prayer,' but you have made it a 'den of thieves.'"
>
> — *Matthew 21:13*

Please read the entire Scripture selection in your own Bible and highlight or underline verses that stand out to you before you read the observations and engage the questions below.

Today we are in Matthew 20–21. We're looking at the time when Jesus not only turned the tables over, but He also turned the tables around on the religious crowd. Our key verse is Matthew 21:13: "And He said to them, 'It is written, "My house shall be called a house of prayer," but you have made it a "den of thieves."'" Now I'm going to focus primarily on chapter 21, which is when Jesus went into Jerusalem. (Actually, in those final days, He went into Jerusalem three times.) But first I want to point out something from the parable in chapter 20 about a landowner and his day laborers.

Let's start with Matthew 20:1–5: "'For the kingdom of heaven is like a landowner who went out early in the morning to hire laborers for his vineyard. Now when he had agreed with the laborers for a denarius a day, he sent them into his vineyard. And he went out about the third hour and saw others standing idle in the marketplace, and said to them, "You also go into the vineyard, and whatever is right I will give you." So they went. Again he went out about the sixth and the ninth hour, and did likewise.'"

The landowner went all the way to the eleventh hour finding laborers, then when the day was done, he paid all the workers the same wage—to the shock of those who had worked *all* day. Then we read in Matthew 20:12–16:

> "These last men have worked only one hour, and you made them equal to us who have borne the burden and the heat of the day." But he answered one of them and said, "Friend, I am doing you no wrong. Did you not agree with me for a denarius? Take what is yours and go your way. I wish to give to this last man the same as to you. Is it not lawful for me to do what I wish with my own things? Or is your eye evil because I am good?" So the last will be first, and the first last. For many are called, but few chosen.

From our current-day perspective, we might protest, "Where's the fairness in this? The ones who worked all day got the same pay as those who worked for just one hour." But here's the reality: they were given what they were promised. The landowner was just. This is the message here: God's goodness and His faithfulness to us is in no way diminished by His grace and generosity to others. The parable of the prodigal son and the response of the older brother contains a similar message. You see, we need to cultivate our hearts so that we're willing to serve, we're grateful for our reward from our Master, and we're able to celebrate His grace poured out on others.

In verses 20–28, the mother of James and John asked Jesus to grant her sons places of honor in His Kingdom. However, Jesus responded by teaching about true greatness, emphasizing that greatness comes from serving others. He explained that He came to serve and give His life as a ransom for many, which echoes Isaiah 53:5–6, 10–12. The point is that instead of seeking positions of authority, we should seek to serve others to the point of sacrifice, just like Jesus. Then in Matthew 20:29–34, we read that as Jesus and His disciples were leaving Jericho, two blind men repeatedly called out to Him for mercy. Notice also how they referred to Him as the messianic Son of David. Despite the crowd's attempts to silence them, Jesus stopped, asked what they wanted, and healed them, restoring their sight. Aside from the compassion Jesus showed them as a model for us all, the point from this story is that, like these blind men, we should be persistent in our faith and not be discouraged by obstacles. Often the Lord rewards persistence as He did here.

Let's move on to chapter 21 where Jesus turned over the tables. Look at verses 12–16:

> Then Jesus went into the temple of God and drove out all those who bought and sold in the temple, and overturned the tables of the money changers and the seats of those who sold doves. And He said to them, "It is written, 'My house shall be called a house of prayer,' but you have made it a 'den of thieves.'" Then the blind and the lame came to Him in the temple, and He healed them. But when the chief priests and scribes saw the wonderful things that He did, and the

> children crying out in the temple and saying, "Hosanna to the Son of David!" they were indignant and said to Him, "Do You hear what these are saying?" And Jesus said to them, "Yes. Have you never read,
>
> 'Out of the mouth of babes and nursing infants
> You have perfected praise'?"

Jesus cleansed the temple of those who, through subterfuge, had turned what was intended to be a sanctuary for prayer and worship of God and a place of help and healing for man into an enterprise of personal profit. So in verse 14, it's interesting what Jesus did. After He cleansed the temple, He healed those who were actually unable to enter—the blind and the lame—so they could then legally enter into the temple, and they could praise and worship God, which is the purpose for which it was intended.

Next, we see the so-called cursing of the fig tree, which took place the next morning. And I believe this illustrates what Jesus did in the temple the day before. Look at Matthew 21:18–22:

> Now in the morning, as He returned to the city, He was hungry. And seeing a fig tree by the road, He came to it and found nothing on it but leaves, and said to it, "Let no fruit grow on you ever again." Immediately the fig tree withered away. And when the disciples saw it, they marveled, saying, "How did the fig tree wither away so soon?" So Jesus answered and said to them, "Assuredly, I say to you, if you have faith and do not doubt, you will not only do what was done to the fig tree, but also if you say to this mountain, 'Be removed and be cast into the sea,' it will be done. And whatever things you ask in prayer, believing, you will receive."

The focus in this passage is generally on the faith required to move mountains and wither fig trees, and we need that faith; however, what do we need that faith for? It's not just moving mountains, not physical mountains.

Think about this for a moment. Jesus was in Bethany, which was next to Bethphage, which means "house of unripe figs." This place was known for its figs. Mark's account actually provides a little more detail that we can draw from here. Jesus saw this fig tree with leaves, which seemed to promise fruit. However, the Scripture says it was not fig season. So it seems maybe that's a little unreasonable to expect figs out of season. But again, if a tree has leaves, it should have figs. Here's the point: the tree boasted of fruit but had none to meet the real and urgent need of Jesus. The religious crowd that He saw the day before had leaves. They had rituals, they had religion, but they were not meeting the needs of the people. As soon as He cleansed the temple, He healed those who needed a touch from God. You see, religion could never meet our deep and profound spiritual need, but a trusting faith in Jesus can bring us into a relationship with God that moves mountains. So it's that faith, that mountain-moving faith of trusting God.

Jesus turned the tables over at the temple, but now let's consider how Jesus turned the tables around. Specifically, how He turned them around on the religious crowd who were seeking to entrap Him. Look at Matthew 21:23–27:

> Now when He came into the temple, the chief priests and the elders of the people confronted Him as He was teaching, and said, "By what authority are You doing these things? And who gave You this authority?" But Jesus answered and said to them, "I also will ask you one thing, which if you

> tell Me, I likewise will tell you by what authority I do these things: The baptism of John—where was it from? From heaven or from men?" And they reasoned among themselves, saying, "If we say, 'From heaven,' He will say to us, 'Why then did you not believe him?' But if we say, 'From men,' we fear the multitude, for all count John as a prophet." So they answered Jesus and said, "We do not know." And He said to them, "Neither will I tell you by what authority I do these things."

See, Jesus knew He could not reason with these men. Their hearts were hardened against Him. And I believe this was an example of what Jesus was saying over in Matthew 7 about not casting your pearls before the swine and using discernment.

Notice how He turned the tables on them by exposing their fears. They didn't fear God. They had a fear of the crowd, so they ended up slinking away after Jesus turned the tables on them. This again reveals the wisdom of Jesus and the confidence and the certainty in which He operated. He did not feel compelled to answer their contrived questions. He simply turned the table on them by asking them questions that exposed the true intent of their heart. A lot of wisdom is here, and this is a good model to follow.

Obviously, there's a lot more in these two chapters, so please read them in their entirety. However, I want to leave you with just one more thought from Matthew 21, and that is from the aftermath of Jesus's parable of the landowner and the wicked tenants (vv. 33–39). In it, Jesus cleverly presented a convicting story of how God sent prophets to His people, but they rejected them, and then He finally sent His Son, whom they killed. Jesus asked in verse 40, "Therefore, when the owner of the vineyard comes, what will he do to those vinedressers?" The religious leaders fell right into Jesus's trap, offering their condemnation, not immediately realizing that they in fact were the "wicked men" in the parable (v. 41). Consequently, in verse 42 Jesus quoted Psalm 118:22–23 then sprung the trap in verse 43:

> "Have you never read in the Scriptures:
> 'The stone which the builders rejected
> Has become the chief cornerstone.
> This was the LORD's doing,
> And it is marvelous in our eyes'?
> "Therefore I say to you, the kingdom of God will be taken from you and given to a nation bearing the fruits of it."

He concludes in Matthew 21:44: "And whoever falls on this stone will be broken; but on whomever it falls, it will grind him to powder." Of course, Jesus was speaking of Himself as the rejected stone who became the chief cornerstone. Now, if this description sounds familiar, it should because you find the prophecy in Daniel 2:34: "You watched while a stone was cut out without hands, which struck the image on its feet of iron and clay, and broke them in pieces."

When Jesus came the first time, He came as a Savior, sent from the Father above, extending grace to those who received Him. Yet the beloved Son was rejected and killed by the very ones He was sent to save. Those who did so fell, broken upon this stone, not cut with hands. You see, we're still living in that dispensation when we can choose our response to Jesus. But when He comes the next time, He will come as the Sovereign, and He will execute judgment upon those who reject His grace and His lordship. Behold, today is the day of salvation.

Questions for Reflection and Discussion

1. What is the point of the parable of the day laborers (see 20:1–16)?
2. In the parable of the wicked tenants, what did they do to the representatives the landowner sent (see 21:33–44)?
   a. Mistreated his servants (i.e., prophets)
   b. Killed his only son (i.e., Jesus)
   c. Both of the above

Notes Today's Bible Reading

— Day 15 —

Today's Reading: Matthew 22–23

Verse of the Day

> And He said to them, "Render therefore to Caesar the things that are Caesar's, and to God the things that are God's."
>
> — *Matthew 22:21*

Please read the entire Scripture selection in your own Bible and highlight or underline verses that stand out to you before you read the observations and engage the questions below.

In today's study we will look at Matthew 22–23. We won't cover every detail in these chapters, but I encourage you to read them. Our key verse is Matthew 22:21, "And He said to them, "Render therefore to Caesar the things that are Caesar's, and to God the things that are God's." The main question I want you to consider is this: As a Christian, what is my responsibility to civil government? We will come back to it in the light of what Jesus said here.

In Matthew 22:1–14 we have the parable of the wedding feast, which is about a king who prepared a wedding banquet for his son. The king sent out his servants with exclusive invitations to chosen guests, and here Jesus alluded to God's chosen people, the Jews, and especially their religious leaders. However, the invited guests refused to come. A second invitation went out, with the urgent message that the banquet was ready, but they ignored the invitation, going about their own business. Some even mistreated and killed the servants, alluding to their treatment of the prophets. Consequently, the king was enraged and sent his army to destroy those murderers and burn their city, which foretells the destruction of Jerusalem in AD 70. Consequently, the king sent his servants into the "highways" to invite everyone, both bad and good, to fill the banquet hall, presumably alluding to the sinners and even the Gentiles. However, once the banquet commenced, the king noticed one guest not wearing the wedding garment he had provided, and the guest was thrown out, symbolizing our need to be properly dressed with the righteousness the Lord Himself provided through the sacrifice of Jesus on the cross.

Next in verses 15–22, the Pharisees tried to trap Jesus with a question about paying taxes to Caesar. Again, we will look at this encounter more in depth later. In verses 23–33, the Sadducees, who did not believe in the resurrection, tried to trap Jesus with a question about marriage in the afterlife. Jesus charged them with not knowing the Scriptures or the power of God and explained that in the resurrection, people will neither marry nor be given in marriage but will be like angels in heaven. In verses 34–40, a Pharisee asked Jesus which commandment is the greatest. Jesus replied that the greatest commandment is to love God with all your heart, soul, and mind, and the second is to love your neighbor as yourself. All the Law and the Prophets hang on these two commandments. Finally in verses 41–46, Jesus turned the tables and questioned the Pharisees about the identity of the Messiah, pointing out that the Messiah is both David's son and Lord, challenging their understanding of the Scriptures.

In Matthew 23:1–12, Jesus addressed the crowds and His disciples and warned them about the hypocrisy of the Pharisees and teachers of the law. The Greek word for "hypocrite" originally came from the realm of theater, where actors in a Greek tragedy or comedy held up masks while performing for the crowds. He criticized these religious leaders for being "play actors," hiding behind their pious masks. He condemned them for not practicing what they preach while at the same time placing heavy burdens on others and not helping to lift them. Jesus instead called for humility, stating that the greatest among them should become their servant. Then in verses 13–36, Jesus pronounced eight "woes" or condemnations against the hypocritical religious leaders:

Woe 1: They shut the door of the kingdom of heaven in people's faces (v. 13).

Woe 2: They devoured widows' houses and for a pretense made long prayers (v. 14).

Woe 3: They made converts who were twice as much children of hell as they were (v. 15).

Woe 4: They swore by the temple and the altar but actually failed to recognize the importance of the temple and the altar (vv. 16–22).

Woe 5: They tithed mint, dill, and cumin but neglected the more important matters of the law, such as justice, mercy, and faithfulness (vv. 23–24).

Woe 6: They cleaned the outside of the cup and dish, but inside they were full of greed and self-indulgence (vv. 25–26).

Woe 7: They were like whitewashed tombs, beautiful on the outside but full of dead bones and everything unclean inside (vv. 27–28).

> Woe 8: They built tombs for the prophets and decorated the graves of the righteous, yet they were the descendants of those who murdered the prophets. That current generation was not only plotting against Jesus, but in the future they also persecuted His followers, as their ancestors did, and they were judged accordingly (vv. 29–36).

Finally, in verses 37–39, Jesus lamented over Jerusalem, expressing deep sorrow for the city's rejection of the prophets and His own message. He spoke of His desire to gather the people as a hen gathers her chicks under her wings, but they were not willing. He predicted their house would be left desolate until they recognized Him as the One who came in the name of the Lord. Once again, Jesus was prophesying about the destruction of Jerusalem in AD 70 and the eventual scattering of the Jewish people. However, another question for us is this: Do we weep over our communities, our cities, our nation like Jesus did? Again, there is much we could apply from this chapter, and I encourage you to spend more time here.

However, let's return to Matthew 22:15–21 where the religious leaders were trying to trap Jesus on the issue of paying taxes, but Jesus once again turned the tables on them. He asked them for a coin then asked whose portrait and inscription was stamped on it (v. 20). They replied, "Caesar's." Jesus responded, "Give to Caesar what is Caesar's and to God what is God's." This is where Jesus began to answer the question what is my responsibility as a Christian to civil government? What am I to give Caesar?

Obviously, we are not citizens living under a Roman regime, yet the principles of stewardship and obligation apply. Americans are blessed to have, as Abraham Lincoln put it, a "government of the people, by the people, for the people."[6] Ever noticed that the original parchment of the Constitution begins "We the People" in big, bold letters? Our form of government requires our active involvement. In fact, Maryland delegate James McHenry told of an encounter Ben Franklin had with a Mrs. Powel, a grand lady of Philadelphia, as the Constitutional Convention ended in 1787: "Well Doctor what have we got, a Republic or a monarchy?" she asked the oldest of the Founding Fathers. You can almost see the twinkle in his eye as he peered over his spectacles and quipped: "A Republic, if you can keep it."[7] Wise old Ben Franklin knew that Republics were not easy to keep. Consequently, our Republic was designed for participants not spectators. How can we "give to Caesar what is Caesar's" and fulfill our stewardship responsibility as Christians who are citizens in America today? There are numerous applications, but here are five specific responsibilities for every believer:

1. *Pray* for your government. Paul instructed, "First of all, then, I urge that supplications, prayers, intercessions, and thanksgivings be made for all people, for kings and all who are in high positions, that we may lead a peaceful and quiet life, godly and dignified in every way. This is good, and it is pleasing in the sight of God our Savior, who desires all people to be saved and to come to the knowledge of the truth" (1 Tim. 2:1–4 ESV). We are to pray for our president, our congressmen, our judges, our governors, our mayors, our councilmen, our law enforcement officials, and so on—for all who have a place of authority. Why are we given specific instructions to prioritize prayer for whom we call political leaders? It's so that we will have good government so we can live in peace as followers of Christ. But there is an underlying truth here that we should not miss. Our government is shaped by the prayers of God's people or by the absence of those prayers. We must pray that they govern in

agreement with the Word of God, and that is much easier when they know Him as Savior and abide in His Word.

2. *Pay* respect to your government. The apostle Peter instructed in 1 Peter 2:13–17: "Be subject for the Lord's sake to every human institution, whether it be to the emperor as supreme, or to governors as sent by him to punish those who do evil and to praise those who do good. For this is the will of God, that by doing good you should put to silence the ignorance of foolish people. Live as people who are free, not using your freedom as a cover-up for evil, but living as servants of God. Honor everyone. Love the brotherhood. Fear God. Honor the emperor" (ESV).

The Greek word for "submit" means to fall in rank under an authority. Government exists to keep order, and we must submit to the rule of law. Peter said that the authorities are commissioned to punish wrongdoers and commend those who are law abiding and productive citizens (v. 14; cf. Rom. 13:2–5). Then Peter said we are to show these authorities honor or respect (v. 17). Sometimes respecting our government is a tall order. However, if we think it is bad in our day, just think about who was in charge when Peter wrote this: Nero. Ever noticed that we name our sons Peter but our dogs Nero? Nero wasn't exactly an altar boy. In fact, he was a brutal, wicked ruler who was likely responsible for the deaths of both Peter and Paul. Yet God's Word says we are to respect the governmental authority, for if we rebel against it, we are in fact rebelling against the God who ordained it (Rom. 13:1–2). We may not have much respect for the person in the office, but we must respect the office of the person in the place of responsibility.

3. *Protest* your government. The right to peacefully protest is enshrined in the Bill of Rights: "The right of the people peaceably to assemble, and to petition the government for a redress of

grievances" (amendment 1). When the government commands what God condemns, then we are obligated to disobey. For example, when Pharaoh commanded that all the male Hebrew babies were to be put to death at the moment of birth, the midwives responded with civil disobedience, and God blessed them for it (Exod. 1:15–21). When King Darius made a law against praying to anyone but himself, Daniel responded with civil disobedience by continuing to pray to God, and God blessed him by delivering him from the lions (Dan. 6:1–23). When the Christians in Asia Minor were commanded to burn a pinch of incense and swear: "Caesar is Lord," they refused, threw their incense to the ground in defiance, and declared, "Christ is Lord!" Jesus commended them for their civil disobedience (Rev. 2:8–10, 13). Finally, the same Peter who wrote that we should submit to the government's authority and respect the king is the same Peter who boldly told the religious rulers of his day who ordered him to stop preaching Jesus, "We ought to obey God rather than men" (Acts 5:29). Consequently, there is a time for peaceful protest and even civil disobedience. However, the latter should come only as a last resort, after all other solutions have been tried and all other avenues exhausted, especially in America, which was founded upon Judeo-Christian principles and biblical laws. However, if the government commands what God condemns, then we are obligated to disobey.

4. *Pay* taxes to your government. All citizens—including His followers—are obligated to support their government. Paul spoke of the government's responsibility to punish evildoers and instructed: "This is also why you pay taxes, for the authorities are God's servants, who give their full time to governing" (Rom. 13:6 NIV). Be honest. This one hurts, especially come tax time. However, when Jesus was asked about paying taxes, He commanded that we are to

give to Caesar what is Caesar's (Matt. 22:21), and He also led by example. As a matter of fact, He had even sent Peter fishing earlier to hook the one that had the very coin in its mouth to pay the tax for Peter and Himself (Matt. 17:24–27)!

Admittedly, there is a lot of waste, fraud, and questionable spending, especially by the entrenched crowd in Washington, DC. Like the *Titanic*, we have hit a financial iceberg, we are taking on water. And while we are still afloat, some people are having fun throwing snowballs on the deck. Still, we are about to drown under a sea of debt and rising taxes unless drastic measures are taken, and the first one is to stop the spending and borrowing against our children's future. The Bible says, "Let no debt remain outstanding" (Rom. 13:8 NIV), but we are amassing debt at an unsustainable rate.

Now I know what you are thinking. *I've complained but the politicians aren't listening, they don't care, and they are going to do it anyway.* But the great thing about America is that if our elected leaders won't change their political and policy positions to line up with the constitution, then we, the people, can change their geographical positions by voting them out of office and sending them back home. However, when we think with a cool head for a moment, we actually do benefit from some of the goods and services provided by the government. First of all, we have the greatest military force in the world and some of the finest young men and women serving in it. We have law enforcement, roads, parks, and so on. So pay your taxes but hold your elected officials accountable for how they spend them. That brings me to the next responsibility to civil government.

5. *Participate* in your government. In America, we have a representative form of government, and you are a part of it. Again, our form of government is intended as a "government of the people, by the people, for the people." Therefore, if we do not actively

participate, then we are not fulfilling the totality of Jesus's command to render to Caesar (Matt. 22:21). It does not make sense that God ordains something (e.g., government), tell us to make it a priority in prayer, and then tells His people to stay out of it. No. God expects us to get involved. After all, if Christians retreat from this arena, then we have allowed Satan to prevail in the very place where Jesus commanded us to make an impact as salt and light. There are many ways we can participate in our government, such as helping with a voter registration drive, commenting on legislation and public policy, speaking out on moral and social issues on social media, holding public office, and volunteering for the election commission.

Perhaps the most basic form of participation is voting—selecting our government. Exodus 18:21 says: "But select capable men from all the people—men who fear God, trustworthy men who hate dishonest gain—and appoint them as officials" (NIV). Voting is a simple act with a significant impact. When we vote, we help determine who will lead our nation, make our laws, and protect our freedoms. Founding father Samuel Adams said, "Let each citizen remember at the moment he is offering his vote . . . that he is executing one of the most solemn trusts in human society for which he is accountable to God and his country."[8] The bottom line is that Christians must vote! Voting is a vital part of our stewardship responsibility. Yet voting for voting's sake is not enough. We need to take it one step further and vote our biblical values. Think about this: Every candidate has his or her own set of values and positions on important issues, issues to which the Bible has principles that have specific application for believers. It is critical that we discover where a candidate stands on the issues and how their values line up with biblical principles. Shouldn't we vote for candidates who share our values? Explaining our U.S. Constitution, John Jay, our nation's first Supreme Court chief justice and one of the three authors of the "Federalist Papers," said, "Providence has given to our people the choice of their rulers, and it is the duty, as well as the privilege and interest of our Christian nation . . . to select and prefer Christians for their rulers."[9]

Unfortunately, many Christians don't even consider biblical values when voting, often choosing candidates whose positions on moral issues are at odds with their own beliefs, convictions, and values, not to mention biblical principle. That's tragic because remember the Lord Jesus expects us to influence and impact, to permeate and penetrate "the earth" and "the world" as the salt and light, which necessarily includes the democratic process. We need to become informed on the issues, know what the candidates stand for and how they vote on issues we care about, read what they say about the issues, check out their online presence, find out who are their enemies and who are their friends, then weigh the candidates' values against biblical values, and prayerfully consider voting for the ones who are the best match. The closer we get to election time, FRCAction.org will be a great place to start.

One caution: Don't allow your involvement with a political party or a politician to usurp your kingdom responsibility. As followers of Christ we need to be unencumbered in our call to speak prophetically to all political parties and politicians. As Dr. Martin Luther King Jr. said in a sermon, entitled "A Knock at Midnight":

> "The church must be reminded once again that [it] is not to be the master or the servant of the state, but the conscience of the state. It must be the guide and the critic of the state,—never its tool. . . . If the church does not recapture

> its prophetic zeal and cease to be an echo of the status-quo it will be relegated to an irrelevant social club with no moral or spiritual authority."[10]

Founding father Benjamin Rush is quoted as saying, "I have been alternately called an Aristocrat and a Democrat. I am neither. I am a Christocrat."[11] Our loyalty must be first, last, and always to the Lord Jesus Christ. So look for statesmen to support, not mere politicians. Politicians think about the next election; statesmen think about the next generation. Strongly consider voting for candidates who most closely align with biblical principles, who believe like you do. Don't just vote to be voting—vote your biblical values! Imagine the impact Christians could have on the direction of our government, the character of its leadership, and the moral health of our nation if we simply applied our biblical worldview and biblical principles to every aspect of our lives—including our participation in government.

One final thought from this passage is the flipside to what Jesus said here in Matthew 22:21, "Give back to Caesar what is Caesar's, *and to God what is God's*" (NIV, emphasis added). We've talked about our obligation to "Caesar," to civil government, but don't miss that last part: We must give to God what belongs to God. While Caesar's image was stamped on the coins, God's image is stamped on us. Paul put it this way in Romans 12:1, "I beseech you therefore, brethren, by the mercies of God, that you present your bodies a living sacrifice, holy, acceptable to God, which is your reasonable service." We are to give Caesar our coins, but we must give God our entire being as an act of worship. Think about that. What would happen if every believer in America gave to God what belongs to God? What if every believer obeyed the two greatest commandments according to Jesus (Matt. 22:37–40): Love God with all our heart, soul, and mind and our neighbor as ourselves? Under God, we could literally see our lives transformed, our families transformed, our communities transformed, and yes, even America transformed. May God make it so!

Questions for Reflection and Discussion

1. In Jesus's answer to the religious leaders about paying taxes to the Roman government, what principles might apply to our patriotic duty as citizens in America (see 22:15–22)?
   a. Support our government (see Matt. 17:24–27; Rom. 13:5–7)
   b. Seek God for our government leaders (see 1 Tim. 2:1–4)
   c. Submit to our government leaders and laws (see 1 Pet. 2:13–14; Rom. 13:2–5)
   d. Stand up to our government when it condemns what God commands or commands what God condemns (see Acts 5:29)
   e. All of the above

2. What did Jesus desire for Jerusalem (see 23:37–39)?

Notes on Today's Bible Reading

— Day 16 —

Today's Reading: Matthew 24

Verse of the Day

> "Watch therefore, for you do not know what hour your Lord is coming."
>
> — *Matthew 24:42*

Please read the entire Scripture selection in your own Bible and highlight or underline verses that stand out to you before you read the observations and engage the questions below.

When we come to Matthew 24, there is a shift. Most of Jesus's teachings up to this point were practical guidance, instruction for Kingdom living. In this chapter, we see Jesus moved into a more prophetic message about the future but with practical application for the present. Our key verse is 42: "'Watch therefore, for you do not know what hour your Lord is coming.'" Parallel accounts of this passage can be found in both Mark 13 and Luke 21. By this point, Jesus had left the temple for the final time; similar to the glory departing the temple in Ezekiel, we see Jesus here walked out. Three days later, the veil of the temple was torn. Forty years later, the temple was destroyed and never rebuilt.

Outside the temple, the disciples were admiring the majestic building when Jesus shocked them with the prediction that it would be destroyed, which prompted them to ask three questions: (1) When will these things be that He was talking about? (2) What will be the signs of His coming? And (3) What will be the signs of the end of the age? Some scholars say Jesus answered two of the three questions, but I think He provided an indirect answer to the third as well. What will be the signs of the ends of the age? That's found in Matthew 24:4–28. What will be the signs of your coming? The answer to that is found in verses 29–31. And what and when will these things be? I think we get a little hint there in verses 42–44.

As we look at this prophetic discourse of Jesus, there's a couple of things to keep in mind. Biblical prophecy generally has multiple horizons. There is the immediate, the intermediate, and the final fulfillment. I suggest this passage has the immediate fulfillment in the destruction of Jerusalem, just forty years after Jesus spoke these words. The events leading up to that destruction were a part of this prophetic message. I think that's quite clear. There is an application beyond that, though, to the church period, as we move toward the great tribulation. And then final fulfillment is in the second coming of Jesus Christ as He sets up His earthly reign.

It is also important to state that doctrinally solid Bible scholars and teachers can disagree on interpretation, and there are several different views on this passage, especially where it pertains to the end times. Again, I do not claim to be an expert in biblical prophecy and especially eschatology. While I've been a student of Scripture for fifty years, I do not claim to have mastered it, nor do I have complete understanding. Some aspects of Scripture, however, are abundantly clear, and one is the doctrine of salvation—the forgiveness of our sins that comes by grace through faith in Jesus Christ alone. Another is the doctrine of sanctification—the work of the

Spirit of God progressively transforming us to be more like Jesus, a people who is called to function as salt and light in this ever-increasingly dark and decaying world. There are other undeniable, irrefutable but also understandable truths and doctrines of Scripture, but the interpretation of end-times prophecy is often open to interpretation. Paul wrote, "For we know in part and we prophesy in part. But when that which is perfect has come, then that which is in part will be done away. . . . For now we see in a mirror, dimly, but then face to face. Now I know in part, but then I shall know just as I also am known" (1 Cor. 13:9–10, 12). Back then a mirror could be nothing more than a polished piece of metal, so all you got was a dim reflection. Similarly, we just don't have the clarity that we will have when it comes to prophecy. Consequently, I caution against taking dogmatic stances on interpretations and especially timelines associated with end-times prophecy.

With all that in mind as background, look at Matthew 24:1–3: "Then Jesus went out and departed from the temple, and His disciples came up to show Him the buildings of the temple. And Jesus said to them, 'Do you not see all these things? Assuredly, I say to you, not one stone shall be left here upon another, that shall not be thrown down.' Now as He sat on the Mount of Olives, the disciples came to Him privately, saying, 'Tell us, when will these things be? And what will be the sign of Your coming, and of the end of the age?'" Again, note those three questions.

Interestingly, Jesus began His response to their questions with a warning in verse 4: "'Take heed that no one deceives you.'" Now it's interesting. They ask, "Hey, when are these things going to be?" And Jesus started off by saying, "Don't be deceived." Three times in this conversation He warned of deception and false prophets, and keep in mind the warning was in the context of the end of the age and Jesus's return. He warned there would be false christs or messiahs coming in His name. In fact, the Jewish historian Josephus recorded several actual imposters in this period between Jesus's ascension into heaven and the destruction of Jerusalem in AD 70.* And this was not only the false christs who came, but it also had application to those who were false saviors or deliverers of the people seeking to supplant the authority and sovereignty of God. In verse 11, Jesus said many false prophets would rise in the time of persecution deceiving many. Now these preach a message counter to the Word of God, seeking to alleviate the conflict with the culture by compromising the truth. And we see today that we have false prophets even in so-called Christian churches.

Now let's go to verse 24: "'For false christs and false prophets will rise and show great signs and wonders to deceive, if possible, even the elect.'" That's pretty intense. The deception is intense. Take note of just how significant the deception is: If possible, even the elect would be deceived. There would be false christs who deceive people. Consider what Paul wrote in 2 Thessalonians 2:9–12: "The

---

* Josephus mentions a dozen or more messianic figures both before and after Jesus's ministry. The following chronological list from Josephus' writings is not exhaustive:

- Hezekiah/Ezekias, defeated by Herod in 47 BC (*Jewish War* 1.204–205)
- Judas (a.k.a. Theudas) son of Ezekias, 4 BC (*Jewish War* 2.56; Acts 5:36)
- Simon of Perea, 4 BC (*Jewish War* 2.57–59)
- Athronges the Shepherd, 4 BC (*Jewish War* 2:60–65)
- Judas the Galilean, AD 6 (*Jewish War* 2.118)
- Theudas, c. AD 44 (*Jewish Antiquities* 20.97; Acts 5:36)
- James and Simon, c. AD 46, sons of Judas the Galilean, crucified by Tiberius Alexander, nephew of Philo, who was procurator AD 46–48 (*Jewish Antiquities* 20.102)
- "The Egyptian" c. AD 50s (*Jewish Antiquities* 20.169–171; *Jewish War* 2.261–263; Acts 21:38)
- Eleazar, son of Dineus/Deinaeus, c. AD 52, under Felix (*Jewish War* 2.253; *Jewish Antiquities* 20:161)
- Menachem, son of Judas the Galilean, AD 66 (*Jewish War* 2:433–448)
- Eleazar, son of Jairus (ben Yair), commander of Masada, was of the family (γένος) of Menachem (*Jewish War* 2.447).

coming of the lawless one is according to the working of Satan, with all power, signs, and lying wonders, and with all unrighteous deception among those who perish, because they did not receive the love of the truth, that they might be saved. And for this reason God will send them strong delusion, that they should believe the lie, that they all may be condemned who did not believe the truth but had pleasure in unrighteousness."

What is truth? In John 14:6, Jesus said, "I am the way, the truth, and the life." How do we dwell in the truth so that we are not deceived? Well, in John 17:17, Jesus prayed this to the Father for us: "Sanctify them by Your truth. Your word is truth." This is the main reason for Stand on the Word. Followers of Jesus Christ must be abiding in Christ, meaning daily in His Word, or they will be the target for Satan's forces of deception. And that's why we must be in the Word of God.

Continue to Matthew 24:6: "'And you will hear of wars and rumors of wars. See that you are not troubled; for all these things must come to pass, but the end is not yet.'" There is a reason that Jesus told us these things are going to happen. Look at John 16:33, "'These things I have spoken to you, that in Me you may have peace. In the world you will have tribulation; but be of good cheer, I have overcome the world.'" So Jesus told His disciples as He's telling us this so that we won't be disturbed by it. We'll know what's unfolding; we'll know that it's happening just as Jesus said it would. And even in the midst of these turbulent times, we can have peace because we are standing firm on the promises and the Word of God.

Read further in Matthew 24:7–8: "'For nation will rise against nation, and kingdom against kingdom. And there will be famines, pestilences, and earthquakes in various places. All these are the beginning of sorrows.'" So do we see these things today? Yes, these are the beginning of sorrows. Let's continue in verses 9–10: "'Then they will deliver you up to tribulation and kill you, and you will be hated by all nations for My name's sake. And then many will be offended, will betray one another, and will hate one another.'" When the persecution of believers begins, so will the falling away, the apostasy. When the trouble begins, Christians will be blamed for causing many of the problems, and that will cause some to turn away from public acknowledgment of Jesus. We saw this during the Covid pandemic where churches were accused of gathering for super-spreader events. They were shut down while casinos and abortion clinics and liquor stores continued to operate. Nero blamed the Christians for the fire that destroyed Rome.

In verse 12, Jesus continued: "And because lawlessness will abound, the love of many will grow cold." As the influence of the church recedes, which keeps the lawlessness in check, lawlessness will abound, and we'll see a cultural tailspin begin. But note what it says here: the love of *many*, but not *all*, will grow cold. Look at verses 13–14: "But he who endures to the end shall be saved. And this gospel of the kingdom will be preached in all the world as a witness to all the nations, and then the end will come." In the immediate fulfillment of this prophecy, the apostles took the Gospel as the persecution in Jerusalem scattered the Jewish people. So the Gospel did go to the then-known world prior to the destruction of Jerusalem. And once again, the Gospel is about to reach every people group around the globe today.

Let's continue in verse 15. Jesus said, "Therefore when you see the 'abomination of desolation,' spoken of by Daniel the prophet, standing in the holy place (whoever reads, let him understand)." Now this is the midpoint in the great tribulation when the antichrist takes off the mask and breaks the agreement with the Jewish people. We read about this in Revelation. We also read about it in Daniel where the antichrist breaks this agreement with the Jewish people and then he defiles the temple, setting himself up to be the one who is to be worshipped. And then he persecutes and even kills those who refuse to yield to him. Daniel prophesied about this (see 8:9–12; 11:21–35). The more immediate fulfillment of Daniel's prophecy was in the person and exploits of Antiochus IV "Epiphanes," who was a type of antichrist, in 175–64 BC. However, there remains an ultimate fulfillment in the one who is yet to come.

So let's look at Matthew 24:29–31:

> "Immediately after the tribulation of those days the sun will be darkened, and the moon will not give its light; the stars will fall from heaven, and the powers of the heavens will be shaken. Then the sign of the Son of Man will appear in heaven, and then all the tribes of the earth will mourn, and they will see the Son of Man coming on the clouds of heaven with power and great glory. And He will send His angels with a great sound of a trumpet, and they will gather together His elect from the four winds, from one end of heaven to the other."

Now let's look at Luke's account of this same thing to help us understand when this will be. Look at Luke 21:24–28:

> "And they will fall by the edge of the sword, and be led away captive into all nations. And Jerusalem will be trampled by Gentiles until the times of the Gentiles are fulfilled. And there will be signs in the sun, in the moon, and in the stars; and on the earth distress of nations, with perplexity,

> the sea and the waves roaring; men's hearts failing them from fear and the expectation of those things which are coming on the earth, for the powers of the heavens will be shaken. Then they will see the Son of Man coming in a cloud with power and great glory. Now when these things begin to happen, look up and lift up your heads, because your redemption draws near."

We are still in the times of the Gentiles. This began with the Babylonian captivity and has continued. It will not end until Jesus returns and sets up His earthly reign at the end of the great tribulation. So this suggests that Matthew 24:29–31 relates to the second coming of Jesus Christ, not the rapture, because the church will have been raptured prior to the completion of the great tribulation.

Jesus continued answering their questions with a parable in verses 32–36:

> "Now learn this parable from the fig tree: When its branch has already become tender and puts forth leaves, you know that summer is near. So you also, when you see all these things, know that it is near—at the doors! Assuredly, I say to you, this generation will by no means pass away till all these things take place. Heaven and earth will pass away, but My words will by no means pass away. But of that day and hour no one knows, not even the angels of heaven, but My Father only."

Jesus said this generation will by no means pass away until all of these things take place. So does that mean all of those He was talking to saw all of this unfold? The Greek word for generation cannot only refer to a set period of time, a generation of thirty to forty years, but it can also mean a nation. So there are a couple of ways to interpret this statement that Jesus made. The initial or near-term fulfillment of this prophecy would have occurred during the lifetimes of those present. That's one way to look at it. Also, if the Word is referring to a nation, a promise that the Jewish nation would be preserved through the times of tribulation and would see the final fulfillment of this prophecy. That interpretation certainly has merit, considering we've seen repeated efforts to exterminate the Jewish people.

Jesus then offered additional descriptions of what the culture, the world, will be like at the time of His return, as we see here in verses 37–39, "But as the days of Noah were, so also will the coming of the Son of Man be. For as in the days before the flood, they were eating and drinking, marrying and giving in marriage, until the day that Noah entered the ark, and did not know until the flood came and took them all away, so also will the coming of the Son of Man be." The time of Noah was an exceedingly wicked time of lawlessness and immorality. Mankind had fallen away from the acknowledgment of God and the worship of God. Noah's warnings to his fellow human beings were ridiculed, and they were rejected. But then suddenly, the rains came and judgment came upon the entire world because it was so wicked. So, Jesus said, "So as it was in the days of Noah, so will it be when the Son of Man returns."

That brings me to the key life application for all of us in verse 42, "Watch therefore, for you do not know what hour your Lord is coming." That's the bottom line. We don't know exactly when He will return, so we need to be living ready. That means we should be in His Word and walking with Him. We need to confess our sins and stay in close fellowship with Him. We should be faithfully serving the Lord and sharing Jesus with others. Consequently, we need to be constantly mindful that the Lord is coming back, and we want Him to catch us serving Him and advancing His kingdom.

Let's finish up with Matthew 24:43–44: "'But know this, that if the master of the house had known what hour the thief would come, he would have watched and not allowed his house to be broken into. Therefore you also be ready, for the Son of Man is coming at an hour you do not expect.'" These verses remind me of a time years ago when I was in law enforcement, as a deputy, working a stakeout in a business that had been robbed. The owner was anticipating that the thief might strike again. So night after night in the early morning hours, we waited and watched. Then finally it happened one night when we caught the guy breaking in, and it turned out to be the owner's brother-in-law, who was in competition with him. Yet he would have been successful, if we had not been waiting and watching at the time he came back. Jesus said the same thing. If the master of the house had known what hour the thief was coming, he would have been waiting at that time. So He said, "Be watchful, because I am coming back."

Questions for Reflection and Discussion

1. What is the correct sequence or timeline of the following end-time events in verses 15–31?
   a. Son of Man (Christ) returns on clouds of glory (v. 30).
   b. Angels gather the elect, the saved (v. 31).
   c. Abomination of desolation (antichrist) appears (v. 15).
   d. Great tribulation takes place (v. 21).

2. Who alone knows "that day and hour" of the end (see v. 36)?

Notes on Today's Bible Reading

— Day 17 —

Today's Reading: Matthew 25

Verse of the Day

> His lord said to him, "Well done, good and faithful servant; you were faithful over a few things, I will make you ruler over many things. Enter into the joy of your lord."
>
> —*Matthew 25:21*

Please read the entire Scripture selection in your own Bible and highlight or underline verses that stand out to you before you read the observations and engage the questions below.

Today we study Matthew 25, which is a continuation of Jesus speaking about preparation for the future with three additional teachings about how to conduct ourselves in the present until He comes. First is the parable of the ten virgins in verses 1–13, then second is the parable of the talents in verses 14–30, then third is what some refer to as the parable of the sheep and goats in verses 31–46, but more on that in a moment. Our key verse is from Matthew 25:21, "His master said to him, 'Well done, good and faithful servant. You have been faithful over a little; I will set you over much. Enter into the joy of your master.'"

First is the parable of the ten virgins in Matthew 25:1–13. Again, in this story Jesus illustrated the importance of being prepared for His return. In the parable, ten virgins were waiting for the bridegroom to arrive for a wedding feast. When the bridegroom arrived unexpectedly at midnight, the five virgins who had extra oil for their lamps were ready for the bridegroom's arrival and entered the wedding feast with him. However, the five who ran out of oil left to buy more. While they were gone, the bridegroom arrived, and they missed out. Interestingly, all were bridesmaids, all had lamps, all expected to meet the bridegroom, and all slept. Outwardly, there appeared to be no difference. Today all may appear to have an outer form of Christianity and profess expectation to meet Christ when He comes. You know a lot of people are on the church rolls who profess Christ but who do not possess Christ. They are not true followers. They may have responded to an invitation, they may have submitted to water baptism, they may have been added to the membership, and they may even serve in the ministries of the church and maybe even on staff!

Yet the Lord Jesus makes a basic distinction in His parable. Some were sensible and others were senseless. Some were prudent and others were imprudent. Some were wise and some were foolish. What basic distinction decided their fate? Some had oil. Some did not. Now those who had oil were not wise because they had oil; they had oil because their lives had a deeper wisdom. They knew they needed to be prepared because they wanted to be ready for the arrival of the bridegroom. They did everything they could so that they would be present to greet Him. So it is with the genuine believer, the faithful follower.

Jesus concluded in verse 13 with a warning to keep watch because we do not know the day or the hour of His return. Consequently, this parable simply reinforces the message at the end of the previous chapter to watch and be ready. Our English word *watch* speaks of a passive attitude. We watch a ballgame. We watch the news. We watch silly reels on social media. While our word is more passive, the Greek word used here in verse 13 means to be actively vigilant, on the edge with preparedness, on high alert. It means to live in a state of readiness. That's the posture of a faithful follower of Jesus.

In verses 14–30 we come to the second parable, the parable of the talents. Of course, the reference to "talent" meant a large sum of money. A Roman talent of gold weighed 57 pounds. In Jesus's day, it was worth about $30,000. Today it would be worth more than $2.8 million! This parable is similar to the one Jesus told in Luke, although there are some differences. Look at verses 14–15: "'For the kingdom of heaven is like a man traveling to a far country, who called his own servants and delivered his goods to them. And to one he gave five talents, to another two, and to another one, to each according to his own ability; and immediately he went on a journey.'" In this parable, the master gave differing amounts of money to the servants based on his assessment of their skill level. However, in the parable in Luke's Gospel, the servants were all given the same amount. Yet in both parables the master expected a return on investment. Let's continue in Matthew 25:16–21:

> "Then he who had received the five talents went and traded with them, and made another five talents. And likewise he who had received two gained two more also. But he who had received one went and dug in the ground, and hid his lord's money. After a long time the lord of those servants came and settled accounts with them. So he who had received five talents came and brought five other talents,

> saying, 'Lord, you delivered to me five talents; look, I have gained five more talents besides them.' His lord said to him, 'Well done, good and faithful servant; you were faithful over a few things, I will make you ruler over many things. Enter into the joy of your lord.'"

The same thing happened with the servant who had two talents and gained two more through business deals. The faithfulness of these servants was rewarded not only with words of affirmation but also with added responsibility.

But then we come to the third servant, the one who did nothing with what he was given. Look at verses 26–30:

> "But his lord answered and said to him, 'You wicked and lazy servant, you knew that I reap where I have not sown, and gather where I have not scattered seed. So you ought to have deposited my money with the bankers, and at my coming I would have received back my own with interest. So take the talent from him, and give it to him who has ten talents. For to everyone who has, more will be given, and he will have abundance; but from him who does not have, even what he has will be taken away. And cast the unprofitable servant into the outer darkness. There will be weeping and gnashing of teeth.'"

What is the application here for us? Well, I think we first have to look at it in the context of Jesus's discourse about the end times and His kingdom. And again, this is where I want to bring in the parable from Luke 19. I believe as His followers, we are left here on the earth as His servants not simply to look after His kingdom as caretakers but as those who would actually expand His holdings and advance His agenda. He expects us not just to be treading water but to be gaining ground. When He returns, we will give an account of what we have done with what we have been given. Some have been given great opportunities, big platforms. Some are only quiet prayer warriors. It doesn't matter what we've been given; it's what we do with what we've been given, and the reward is proportional. If you have been faithful with what you've been given, you will be rewarded.

Consequently, here's my takeaway from this. While the work that we do in this life is temporal, the reward is eternal. What we do in this life will set the stage for what we're able to do throughout all eternity. Now to be clear, this has nothing to do with our salvation but rather service to the Lord. Eternity in the new heaven and new earth is going to be a place we're able to actually use our gifts and our abilities to serve the Lord. We're not going to be floating around on clouds. It's not going to be a perpetual church service. We're going to be working, especially in the millennial Kingdom. We will be reigning with the Lord, and we will be working for Him and with Him.

I believe what we will see is that to the degree we're faithful with what God has given us in this life, facing opposition and difficulties in this fallen world, we're then going to be able to use our giftings and our passions truly unopposed in eternity to do what God created us to do. And from that is going to come great joy. We know that God works. He was working before time. He was working when He created the earth. God is not idle, and I don't think we're going to be idle either. Before the fall of man, what was Adam doing in the garden? He was working. There is great joy in work. And so, I think what we see here is that our faithfulness in this life determines our positioning to serve the Lord in the life to come, which is all eternity.

The remainder of Matthew 25 in verses 31–46 some take as a parable. Some call it the parable of the sheep and goats, while others call it the parable of the final judgment. However, there is no introductory indicator like we have with other parables (e.g., "The kingdom of heaven is like"). Consequently, others believe this passage is simply a description of the final judgment. Regardless, the takeaways are the same. Let's look at verses 31–32, "When the Son of Man comes in His glory, and all the holy angels with Him, then He will sit on the throne of His glory. All the nations will be gathered before Him, and He will separate them one from another, as a shepherd divides his sheep from the goats." The line of separation comes down to how they treated the needy, the suffering, the "least of these" (v. 45).

Jesus teaches us that genuine faith is demonstrated through our actions toward others, serving, showing compassion, and meeting needs. Indeed, how we treat others in need has a direct correlation to how we regard Jesus Himself: "inasmuch as you did it to one of the least of these My brethren, you did it to Me" (v. 40). In fact, John put it this way in 1 John 4:20–21: "If anyone says, 'I love God,' and hates his brother, he is a liar; for he who does not love his brother whom he has seen cannot love God whom he has not seen. And this commandment we have from him: whoever loves God must also love his brother" (ESV). Acts of kindness toward the needy, no matter how small, are significant in the eyes of the Lord and are proof of our love for Him.

So we read here of King Jesus, sitting on His glorious throne in judgment, and we read of two verdicts with two diametrically opposite destinations. Those who closed their hearts and refused to help, "will go away into everlasting punishment," while those who showed compassion toward the vulnerable are deemed as the "righteous" who will go "into eternal life" (v. 46). This teaching should serve as a sobering reminder that how we treat others either proves or denies our faith, and it matters so much to God that it determines destiny. What a motivation to live with an eternal perspective, understanding that our faith in action has eternal consequences!

Questions for Reflection and Discussion

1. What is the point of the parable of the ten virgins (vv. 1–13)?

2. In the parable of the final judgment what type of behavior did Jesus describe that will divide the sheep from the goats (vv. 31–46)?
   a. Met the needs of the hungry and thirsty
   b. Welcomed the stranger
   c. Clothed the naked
   d. Visited the sick and imprisoned
   e. All of the above

Notes on Today's Bible Reading

— Day 18 —

Today's Reading: Matthew 26

Verse of the Day

> Again, a second time, He went away and prayed, saying, "O My Father, if this cup cannot pass away from Me unless I drink it, Your will be done."
>
> — *Matthew 26:42*

Please read the entire Scripture selection in your own Bible and highlight or underline verses that stand out to you before you read the observations and engage the questions below.

Today we begin the passion, the suffering of Jesus as we read Matthew 26, the longest chapter in the book of Matthew. Our key verse is 42: "Again, a second time, He went away and prayed, saying, 'O My Father, if this cup cannot pass away from Me unless I drink it, Your will be done.'" This chapter covers a lot, so let's get started with verses 1–2: "Now it came to pass, when Jesus had finished all these sayings, that He said to His disciples, 'You know that after two days is the Passover, and the Son of Man will be delivered up to be crucified.'" This follows Jesus's prophetic discourse we read in chapters 24–25. It was now Wednesday, and Jesus said He would be betrayed, and on Friday, which was Passover, He would be crucified. Let's continue in 26:3–5: "Then the chief priests, the scribes, and the elders of the people assembled at the palace of the high priest, who was called Caiaphas, and plotted to take Jesus by trickery and kill Him. But they said, 'Not during the feast, lest there be an uproar among the people.'" Now don't miss this. The so-called religious leaders wanted to avoid killing Jesus during Passover for fear of creating a riot among the people. This is more evidence that Jesus's life was not taken from Him, but He gave it, and we're going to see even more proof.

The leaders did not want to kill Jesus during the Passover, but He died on the cross on the same day that the Passover lambs were being slain in the temple. Coincidence? No. The Passover pointed back to the deliverance from Egypt, when the angel of death passed over their homes, and it looked forward to the Messiah, the Passover Lamb. This next event actually occurred four days prior to the first part of this chapter. So this one event is not in chronological order.

Let's continue in verse 6: "And when Jesus was in Bethany at the house of Simon the leper." We don't know anything else about Simon, but it's obvious that he's no longer a leper because he's hosting Jesus and others. So it's very likely that Jesus had healed him and restored him to fellowship with his family and his community. Next read verse 7: "A woman came to Him having an alabaster flask of very costly fragrant oil, and she poured it on His head as He sat at the table." From John's account, we know this was Mary, who was the sister of Martha and Lazarus, who were at the dinner along with others. In Mark's account, he actually lists the cost of this oil, which was roughly a year's wages. Look at Matthew 26:8–9: "But when His disciples saw it, they were indignant, saying, 'Why this waste? For this fragrant oil might have been sold for much and given to the poor.'" Now, there have been many self-enriching actions taken in the name of the poor. John told us Judas was the one who raised the objections here, and he happened to be the one who held the money bag. He was the one who held the money for the group.

Let's continue in Matthew 26:10–11: "But when Jesus was aware of it, He said to them, 'Why do you trouble the woman? For she has done a good work for Me. For you have the poor with you always, but Me you do not have always.'" The main message here was concern for the poor was not an excuse to not worship the Lord. There would be other opportunities to serve the poor. And I think this is also an acknowledgment that material poverty would not be eliminated until spiritual poverty was eradicated. As long as there sin in the world, Jesus said, there's going to be poverty. Now read verses 14–15: "Then one of the twelve, called Judas Iscariot, went to the chief priests and said, 'What are you willing to give me if I deliver Him to you?' And they counted out to him thirty pieces of silver." Let's jump to verse 17: "Now on the first day of the Feast of the Unleavened Bread the disciples came to Jesus, saying to Him, 'Where do You want us to prepare for You to eat the Passover?'"

At this time, let's review the order of events from this point forward based on all four Gospels because Matthew only offered the basic facts. And when we look at all the Gospels together, we get a more comprehensive picture of the events.

1. Jesus washed the feet of the disciples.
2. Jesus identified Judas as the betrayer.
3. Judas left the dinner, the Lord's Supper.
4. The Lord's Supper was instituted. This was after they eat. He passed the bread, the wine.
5. Jesus had a conversation in the upper room.
6. Then there's the discourse on the way to Gethsemane.

7. Jesus prayed for His disciples and those who would believe based upon their testimony. That's us. That's in John 17.
8. Jesus was in prayer and anguish in Gethsemane.
9. Jesus was betrayed and arrested.

Let's go back and focus on the events Matthew reports, beginning with the Passover meal and what Jesus did with it in 26:26–28: "And as they were eating, Jesus took bread, blessed and broke it, and gave it to the disciples and said, 'Take, eat; this is My body.' Then He took the cup, and gave thanks, and gave it to them, saying, 'Drink from it, all of you. For this is My blood of the new covenant, which is shed for many for the remission of sins.'" What Jesus said here echoed Isaiah 53:5–6, 12:

> But He was wounded for our transgressions,
> He was bruised for our iniquities;
> The chastisement for our peace was upon Him,
> And by His stripes we are healed.
> All we like sheep have gone astray;
> We have turned, every one, to his own way;
> And the LORD has laid on Him the iniquity of us all. . . .
> Therefore I will divide Him a portion with the great,
> And He shall divide the spoil with the strong,
> Because He poured out His soul unto death,
> And He was numbered with the transgressors,
> And He bore the sin of many,
> And made intercession for the transgressors.

Remember, Matthew highlighted the many ways Jesus is the fulfillment of messianic prophecy—and in this case Isaiah's Suffering

Servant predicted more than 700 years before His coming. The larger point is that our commemoration of the Lord's Supper is to be a reminder of the new covenant brought about by His death, burial, and resurrection.

Let's continue in Matthew 26:29: "'But I say to you, I will not drink of this fruit of the vine from now on until that day when I drink it new with you in My Father's kingdom.'" So, the scholars believe this is the millennial Kingdom. When Jesus comes back to reign on this earth. Look at verse 31: "Then Jesus said to them, 'All of you will be made to stumble because of Me this night, for it is written: "I will strike the Shepherd, And the sheep of the flock will be scattered."'" Again, this is from Zechariah 13:7. Continue down to Matthew 26:33–34: "Peter answered and said to Him, 'Even if all are made to stumble because of You, I will never be made to stumble.' Jesus said to him, 'Assuredly, I say to you that this night, before the rooster crows, you will deny Me three times.'" In verses 36–46, we have Jesus's travail in the garden. It's His human will versus divine will and Jesus's submission to God the Father. Look at verse 42: "Again, a second time, He went away and prayed, saying, 'O My Father, if this cup cannot pass away from Me unless I drink it, Your will be done.'" Three times Jesus prayed to the Father as He faced carrying the sin of humanity to the cross and experiencing the separation from the Father.

Verses 47–56 cover His arrest, which is recorded in the Gospel of Luke in greater detail. After Judas betrayed Jesus with a kiss, the Jewish guards sent from the religious leaders moved in to arrest Jesus. In his rash attempt to protect Jesus, Peter pulled out his sword and lopped off the ear of Malchus, the servant of the high priest, but he intended to do more damage than that (John 18:10). He just wasn't a very good swordsman. Jesus stayed Peter's hand

and ordered him, "Put your sword back into its place, for all who take the sword will perish by the sword." That is the biblical origin of the popular proverb "live by the sword, die by the sword." Yet notice what Jesus told Peter about his sword: "Put your sword back into its place," in his belt or a scabbard at his side. Notice that Jesus did not say, "turn it into the government" or "give it away" or "throw it away." The Lord Jesus said, "Put it in its place." So a weapon has a place in the life of a believer for self-defense, the defense of family and friends, and the defense of country. You might say that Peter received his "Carry License" from Jesus Himself. And by extension, we have the same right.

Yet this was a rebuke from the Lord. We are not to use the sword in order to attempt to advance God's kingdom. In fact, Jesus later told Pilate in John 18:36, "My kingdom is not of this world. If my kingdom were of this world, my servants would have been fighting, that I might not be delivered over to the Jews. But my kingdom is not from the world." In fact, Jesus had a heavenly arsenal at His disposal if needed, as He declared in Matthew 26:53: "Or do you think that I cannot now pray to My Father, and He will provide Me with more than twelve legions of angels?" Remember when one single angelic warrior in Isaiah 37:36–37 took out 185,000 Assyrians? Yet Jesus essentially declared, "Look, I could call down angels to rescue me, but that's not the point." He didn't want an angelic rescue or have Peter lead the disciples to engage in a sword fight against this mob. To do so would be to stand in the way of His crucifixion and undermine God's sovereign plan for Jesus to die a sacrificial death on the cross for the sins of the world. Indeed, this was His destiny as foretold by prophecy: "But how then should the Scriptures be fulfilled, that it must be so?" (v. 54 ESV). What Jesus was saying was, "Peter, I'm going to the cross; this is God's plan as predicted by the prophets, so let it happen without a fight." Consequently, Jesus made clear that His life was not being taken from Him. God was sovereignly orchestrating all of these events to bring about His plan for our salvation. So again, it shows that Jesus's life was not being taken, but it was being given. And that's very important. Remember Matthew 20:28: "just as the Son of Man did not come to be served, but to serve, and to give His life a ransom for many."

Once Jesus was arrested, He had to endure a sham trial before the high priest and his kangaroo court (a.k.a. the Sanhedrin). Look at Matthew 26:57–60: "And those who had laid hold of Jesus led Him away to Caiaphas the high priest, where the scribes and the elders were assembled. But Peter followed Him at a distance to the high priest's courtyard. And he went in and sat with the servants to see the end. Now the chief priests, the elders, and all the council sought false testimony against Jesus to put Him to death, but found none. Even though many false witnesses came forward, they found none. But at last two false witnesses came forward."

They looked for false testimony, and finally, they found two who lied. Now think about this for a moment. Two people bore false witness against God. God's law for the Jewish people to safeguard justice required two or three witnesses to find someone guilty. This is another example of publicly abiding by the letter of the law but secretly violating the intent of the law because justice was not done at the hands of these religious leaders.

Let's continue with this so-called trial in verses 61–64:

> "This fellow said, 'I am able to destroy the temple of God and to build it in three days.'" And the high priest arose and said to Him, "Do You answer nothing? What is it these men testify against You?" But Jesus kept silent. And the

> high priest answered and said to Him, "I put You under oath by the living God: Tell us if You are the Christ, the Son of God!" Jesus said to him, "It is as you said. Nevertheless, I say to you, hereafter you will see the Son of Man sitting at the right hand of the Power, and coming on the clouds of heaven."

You know, throughout this whole ordeal, even as we'll see in the next chapter when He appears before Pilate, Jesus's words were very few so that there was great clarity in what He said. Every word had weight and meaning. He meant what He said, and He said what He meant. Yet here is the response in verse 65: "Then the high priest tore his clothes, saying, "He has spoken blasphemy! What further need do we have of witnesses? Look, now you have heard His blasphemy!"

At the close of this chapter, we have Peter's three encounters: two with servant girls, one with the crowd. Just as Jesus predicted, Peter denied Him all three times. Look at verses 74–75: "Then he began to curse and swear, saying, 'I do not know the Man!' Immediately a rooster crowed. And Peter remembered the word of Jesus who had said to him, 'Before the rooster crows, you will deny Me three times.' So he went out and wept bitterly." Recall in verse 31, Jesus said that all would be made to stumble or fall away. Peter was so bold in saying that he would die with Jesus if need be, and it was a heartfelt declaration. I have no doubt that Peter was "all in" when he said that. They were in the garden with Him praying, and Jesus was disappointed in their inability to stay awake and pray. He pointed out in verse 41, "The spirit indeed is willing, but the flesh is weak." Peter had good intentions, but like him, the reality is we cannot faithfully serve God or stand in the face of the enraged and desperate forces of darkness in our own strength. We must have the power of the Holy Spirit, and later we certainly see Peter lived this out in the pages of the book of Acts.

Questions for Reflection and Discussion

1. At the last Passover supper with His disciples, how did Jesus identify the one who would betray Him (vv. 20–25)?
2. After Peter drew his sword, lopping off the ear of the high priest's armed servant, what did Jesus tell Peter to do with the sword (see vv. 52–54)?
   a. Give your sword to the governing officials.
   b. Get rid of your sword.
   c. Put your sword in its place.
   d. None of the above.

Notes on Today's Bible Reading

— Day 19 —

Reflection on Matthew 18–26

Sunday Reflection and Discussion

Gather with family or friends and use the guide below for a time of prayer, reflection, and discussion:

- Opening Prayer – Praise and a brief prayer for spiritual insight and unity.
- Recap – Briefly summarize Matthew 18–26.
- Discussion Questions – Use open-ended, age-appropriate prompts to spark meaningful worldview conversations. Here are some suggestions:
    1. Most meaningful passage that spoke to you personally?
    2. Insights gained about God: Who He is, What He values and expects, How He works?
    3. Applications that we can make from the Word to what is happening in the world?
    4. How would God have you apply His truth to your life personally?
- Action Steps – Encourage each family member to share a personal takeaway or action step for living the truth revealed in God's Word.
- Closing Prayer – Conclude by praising God for how He has revealed Himself, His purposes, and His ways, and by

praying for His help in living in the light of His truth and sharing it with others during the week ahead.

Additional Notes

— Day 20 —

Today's Reading: Matthew 27

Verse of the Day

> When Pilate saw that he could not prevail at all, but rather that a tumult was rising, he took water and washed his hands before the multitude, saying, "I am innocent of the blood of this just Person. You see to it."
>
> — *Matthew 27:24*

Please read the entire Scripture selection in your own Bible and highlight or underline verses that stand out to you before you read the observations and engage the questions below.

In Matthew 27 we meet a man who was afraid of the people and yet struck by the presence in the disposition of Jesus. But in the end, Pilate tried to wash his hands of Jesus. Our key verse is 24: "When Pilate saw that he could not prevail at all, but rather that a tumult was rising, he took water and washed his hands before the multitude, saying, 'I am innocent of the blood of this just Person. You see to it.'" Combining the narratives of the four Gospels, we can construct a more comprehensive account of the basic facts in what Matthew's Gospel provides.

Jesus was arrested after midnight, so it took a while to assemble the Sanhedrin. In the meantime, Jesus was taken to the house of Annas, the former high priest, who was really kind of a puppet master. So Jesus then was taken to Caiaphas, the sitting high priest, who was the son-in-law of Annas. Jesus then appeared before the full religious council, the Sanhedrin. Because Jewish leaders did not have the authority to actually execute people, He was taken to Pilate, the Roman authority, who found that Jesus is from Galilee. In an attempt to sidestep making a decision, Pilate sent him to Herod Antipas, who was the governor of that region of Galilee. Herod Antipas was the son of Herod the Great, whose kingdom was divided among his three sons when he died. Antipas was given the Galilee region, Philip was given the Gentile area north of Galilee, and Archelaus was actually given the prime area, and that was Judea. However, there were so many problems surrounding Archelaus that Caesar Augustus took the territory from him and established a Roman governorship, Pilate being the fifth Roman governor in the area in Jerusalem and Judea.

To continue with the trials, Herod didn't want to handle the situation, so he sent Jesus back to Pilate, who told the Jewish leaders He was innocent and said he would punish Jesus and release Him. But the priests balked at the offer. A crowd built and Pilate offered then to release a prisoner, which was customary at the time of the Passover. Instead of taking Jesus, the crowd, coached by the priests, demanded Barabbas. Pilate tried to wash his hands of Jesus. He had Jesus flogged and hoped that satisfied the crowd. It did not. Pilate then, for a third time, tried to persuade the crowd, but they accused him at that point of being disloyal to Rome. He was fearful, so he relented and ordered that Jesus be crucified.

With that overview of the sequence, let's start in Matthew 27:2–4: "And when they had bound Him, they led Him away and delivered Him to Pontius Pilate the governor. Then Judas, His betrayer, seeing that He had been condemned, was remorseful and brought back the thirty pieces of silver to the chief priests and elders, saying, 'I have sinned by betraying innocent blood.' And they said, 'What is that to us? You see to it!'"

They were basically saying, "That's your problem." When Judas realized that Jesus had been condemned to die, he was filled with remorse. That was not really his plan. He took the money back and declared Jesus as innocent. But the religious leaders didn't care. Judas had served their purposes. In fact, we read in verse 5, "Then he threw down the pieces of silver in the temple and departed, and went and hanged himself."

Now some often ask the question, "Could Judas have been forgiven and restored to his relationship with Jesus?" After all, Peter denied Jesus three times, and he too was remorseful. He went out and wept, and we read in John's Gospel that he was restored to fellowship with Jesus. Judas could have been, but he took his own life instead of persevering. Suicide is the means by which Satan often secures the souls of the lost.

Continue in Matthew 27:6: "But the chief priests took the silver pieces and said, 'It is not lawful to put them into the treasury, because they are the price of blood.'" This was hypocrisy. They killed an innocent man, but then they were concerned about putting tainted money into the temple treasury. Jesus's words so accurately described these religious leaders when He said in Matthew 23:24, "Blind guides, who strain out a gnat and swallow a camel!"

In 27:13–14 we read, "Then Pilate said to Him, 'Do You not hear how many things they testify against You?' But He answered him not one word, so that the governor marveled greatly." By the way, Pilate was described in history as an evil, ruthless, and brutal man. Yet he saw something in Jesus that caused him to marvel, which explains why he tried to avoid condemning Jesus to death. Let's continue in verses 15–17: "Now at the feast the governor was accustomed to releasing to the multitude one prisoner whom they wished. And at that time they had a notorious prisoner called Barabbas. Therefore, when they had gathered together, Pilate said to them, 'Whom do you want me to release to you? Barabbas, or Jesus who is called Christ?'"

Let's jump to Matthew 27:20–21: "But the chief priests and elders persuaded the multitudes that they should ask for Barabbas and destroy Jesus. The governor answered and said to them, 'Which of the two do you want me to release to you?' They said, 'Barabbas!'" Think about this for a moment. Barabbas was a notorious criminal, a rebel, and possibly a murderer, an insurrectionist. Consequently, here a guilty man was set free and an innocent man was condemned. You know, we each actually stand in this position of Barabbas. Guilty. Yet we are set free, and Jesus paid the price for our sin.

In fact, we read in verse 26 that they scourged Him, which meant thirty-nine lashes, one less than death, with a Roman *flagellum*, which was a short-handled whip with long leather strips embedded with bits of bone or metal in the ends. Our Lord's back would have been flayed open with every cruel stroke. No doubt it was unbearable. Yet when I think about it, it fills my heart with a mixture of sorrow and gratitude, and it reminds me of Isaiah 53:5: "by His stripes we are healed." Then we read that Pilate "delivered Him to be crucified," but first we read of his mockery and mistreatment by the soldiers in verses 27–31:

> Then the soldiers of the governor took Jesus into the Praetorium and gathered the whole garrison around Him. And

> they stripped Him and put a scarlet robe on Him. When they had twisted a crown of thorns, they put it on His head, and a reed in His right hand. And they bowed the knee before Him and mocked Him, saying, "Hail, King of the Jews!" Then they spat on Him, and took the reed and struck Him on the head. And when they had mocked Him, they took the robe off Him, put His own clothes on Him, and led Him away to be crucified.

What incredible indignity Jesus suffered all because of His great love for us! At this point, Jesus was incapable of carrying His own cross beam, so they compelled Simon, the Cyrene, to carry it up to the place called Golgotha, which was the "Place of a Skull" (vv. 32–33). Then we read the very simple but weighty words in verse 35, "Then they crucified Him."

The four Roman soldiers on this execution detail would have laid Jesus on the cross beam and the support beam and taken iron spikes and driven them into His wrists and ankles, not the hands and feet like the paintings because that would not keep a body in place. Then we read in verse 35 that they "divided His garments, casting lots, that it might be fulfilled which was spoken by the prophet: 'They divided My garments among them, And for My clothing they cast lots'" (see Ps. 22:18). Then the soldiers fixed a sign on the cross in verse 37, "And they put up over His head the accusation written against Him: THIS IS JESUS THE KING OF THE JEWS." Little did they realize the truth of the sign that was meant to accuse and mock.

Further in Matthew 27:39–44 we read that when Jesus was on the cross:

> Those who passed by blasphemed Him, wagging their heads and saying, "You who destroy the temple and build it in three days, save Yourself! If You are the Son of God, come down from the cross." Likewise the chief priests also, mocking with the scribes and elders, said, "He saved others; Himself He cannot save. If He is the King of Israel, let Him now come down from the cross, and we will believe Him. He trusted in God; let Him deliver Him now if He will have Him; for He said, 'I am the Son of God.'" Even the robbers who were crucified with Him reviled Him with the same thing.

So they said, "If you come down from the cross, we'll believe you." Why would they have believed Him then? I mean, considering all of the miracles Jesus had done, one more would not have convinced them. Although He came and He testified, and He did the miracles, they still wouldn't believe; they rejected him. And through His death, burial, and resurrection, the message of God's salvation and redemption has gone around the world. Yet don't miss the caution these mockers provide for us today. Some might say, "Well, you know, if God would just do this, I would believe, or if God would just do that, I would surrender to Him." Remember God has done everything for you. He sent His Son to die for your sins and for my sins. And one more act of God is not going to convince you. It is a choice you must make now.

Halfway through Jesus's ordeal on the cross, it became midnight at midday, as we read in Matthew 27:45–46, "Now from the sixth hour until the ninth hour there was darkness over all the land. And about the ninth hour Jesus cried out with a loud voice, saying, 'Eli, Eli, lama sabachthani?' that is, 'My God, My God, why have

You forsaken Me?'" Those who know the Old Testament will recognize that Jesus's cry from the cross is a quotation from and fulfillment of Psalm 22:1. It is interesting to note that Jesus goes back to the psalms to voice His deepest feelings in the darkness. Yet this cry from Jesus is difficult to understand, at least on the surface. In what sense did God "forsake" Jesus? As God's only begotten Son, God still loved Him. God approved of Jesus and His mission. At His baptism, and again at His transfiguration, God declared from the heavens, "This is My beloved Son, in whom I am well pleased." Further, Jesus was innocent as He suffered and died in the cross. He was sinless, and He fulfilled the law of God and carried out the plan of God perfectly. He had done nothing to forfeit the favor of God. In none of these respects could God have forsaken Him.

The answer is found in the prophecy of Isaiah that was fulfilled by Jesus on the cross, and we looked at these verses earlier:

> Surely He has borne our griefs
> And carried our sorrows;
> Yet we esteemed Him stricken,
> Smitten by God, and afflicted.
> But He was wounded for our transgressions,
> He was bruised for our iniquities;
> The chastisement for our peace was upon Him,
> And by His stripes we are healed.
> All we like sheep have gone astray;
> We have turned, every one, to his own way;
> And the Lord has laid on Him the iniquity of us all.
> (Isa. 53:4–6)

On that cross, Jesus became our substitute. He took our place and our punishment. He endured God's wrath that was due us. He took the hell that was justly coming to us so that we might enjoy His heaven. Peter put it this way in 1 Peter 2:21–24:

> For to this you were called, because Christ also suffered for us, leaving us an example, that you should follow His steps:
>
> > "Who committed no sin,
> > Nor was deceit found in His mouth";
>
> who, when He was reviled, did not revile in return; when He suffered, He did not threaten, but committed Himself to Him who judges righteously; who Himself bore our sins in His own body on the tree, that we, having died to sins, might live for righteousness—by whose stripes you were healed.

Paul made a similar but more succinct statement in 2 Corinthians 5:21, "For He made Him who knew no sin to be sin for us, that we might become the righteousness of God in Him." It was the ultimate manifestation of God's wrath directed toward sin, in a way we can't fully comprehend or explain, that Jesus experienced in that terrible hour, symbolized by that oppressive darkness. On that cross, Jesus somehow sensed such desolation that He was no longer conscious of His Father's presence or His love. So there in the darkness as He bore the sins of the world as a substitute, Jesus felt abandoned by God and took up the lament from Psalm 22:1: "My God, My God, why have You forsaken Me?" As horrible as the physical suffering must have been for Him, this feeling of abandonment by God was even worse. That's at the heart of the cross. That's when He became our substitute and our Savior.

Then we read in verse 50, "And Jesus cried out again with a loud voice, and yielded up His spirit." The Greek word translated *yielded* literally means to "dismiss," like a military officer dismisses his troops, giving them permission to leave. See Jesus did not die a victim of circumstances. Again, His life was not taken. According to the sovereign plan of God, Jesus willingly gave His life, and in the end, He dismissed His spirit.

In the aftermath of His death, consider the amazing events that took place in Matthew 27:51–53: "Then, behold, the veil of the temple was torn in two from top to bottom; and the earth quaked, and the rocks were split, and the graves were opened; and many bodies of the saints who had fallen asleep were raised; and coming out of the graves after His resurrection, they went into the holy city and appeared to many."

The veil of the temple being torn has great symbolism and spiritual significance. That curtain divided the public and even the rank and file priesthood, with the exception of the high priest once a year, from the holy of holies and the presence of Holy God. Notice also it was torn top to bottom, heavenward to earthward, symbolizing God's initiative toward us. Now the way to God was open because of the sacrificial death of Jesus Christ, who made atonement for our sin, and His offering was accepted by Holy God. Honestly, we know very little about this occurrence of saints being raised, other than that it was a testimony to the seismic impact of Jesus's death and three days later His resurrection.

But let's go back to the impact of Jesus's death and the earthquake that followed in Matthew 27:54: "So when the centurion and those with him, who were guarding Jesus, saw the earthquake and the things that had happened, they feared greatly, saying, 'Truly this was the Son of God!'" These were hardened Roman soldiers gripped by the reality of what they saw standing at the foot of the cross.

The remainder of the chapter, verses 57–66, provide a narrative of the burial of Jesus in the tomb of Joseph of Arimathea and guards being set there at the entrance to ensure that Jesus's disciples did not steal the body. Joseph of Arimathea was a prominent member of the Sanhedrin, who would have been present at the trial of Jesus. He was also a secret disciple of Jesus, but when Jesus was crucified, He stepped out of the shadows to publicly request Jesus's body from Pilate and arranged for His body to be buried in his own tomb. What a risk of faith! Joseph's actions demonstrate loyalty to Jesus, even in the face of potential religious, social, and even physical repercussions. His courageous faith at a critical moment should be an inspiration to us in a hostile culture. Next, we will study about the fact that Jesus triumphed over death and came out of Joseph's borrowed tomb as risen Lord.

Questions for Reflection and Discussion

1. What irony is found in the sign hung on the cross, which was intended to mock Jesus (vv. 27–37)?

2. What events happened when Jesus died on the cross and followed His resurrection (vv. 51–53)?
   a. The veil of the temple was torn in two from top to bottom.
   b. The earth quaked, rocks split, and graves opened.
   c. Many dead saints were raised after Christ's resurrection, went into the holy city, and appeared to many.
   d. All of the above.

Notes on Today's Bible Reading

— Day 21 —

Today's Reading: Matthew 28

Verse of the Day

> And Jesus came and spoke to them, saying, "All authority has been given to Me in heaven and on earth.
>
> —*Matthew 28:18*

Please read the entire Scripture selection in your own Bible and highlight or underline verses that stand out to you before you read the observations and engage the questions below.

Today we come to Matthew 28 and conclude our study of the Gospel. Our key verse is Matthew 28:18: "And Jesus came and spoke to them, saying, 'All authority has been given to Me in heaven and on earth.'" In this final chapter, we have Christ conquering the grave, we have critics conspiring to lie, and we have the commissioning of the disciples. It is important to note that both John and Luke's Gospels provide much more of Jesus's forty days between His resurrection and the ascension. In Acts 1:3, Luke reports that Jesus "presented Himself alive after His suffering by many infallible proofs." Paul alludes to the fact that there were more than 500 eyewitness accounts (1 Cor. 15:6). Here in Matthew, we have four powerful proofs of Jesus's resurrection. We have the angels, the women, the guards, and the disciples.

Let's begin in Matthew 28:1–10,

> Now after the Sabbath, as the first day of the week began to dawn, Mary Magdalene and the other Mary came to see the tomb. And behold, there was a great earthquake; for an angel of the Lord descended from heaven, and came and rolled back the stone from the door, and sat on it. His countenance was like lightning, and his clothing as white as snow. And the guards shook for fear of him, and became like dead men. But the angel answered and said to the women, "Do not be afraid, for I know that you seek Jesus who was crucified. He is not here; for He is risen, as He said. Come, see the place where the Lord lay. And go quickly and tell His disciples that He is risen from the dead, and indeed He is going before you into Galilee; there you will see Him. Behold, I have told you." So they went out quickly from the tomb with fear and great joy, and ran to bring His disciples word. And as they went to tell His disciples, behold, Jesus met them, saying, "Rejoice!" So they came and held Him by the feet and worshiped Him. Then Jesus said to them, "Do not be afraid. Go and tell My brethren to go to Galilee, and there they will see Me.'"

Why is the fact that Jesus rose from the dead and conquered the grave so important? It is a fundamental of the Christian faith. As we saw in chapters 26 and 27, Jesus gave His life. He willingly became the object of God's wrath and took upon Himself the sin of all mankind, paying the penalty, as foretold in prophecy. Yet He didn't stay in the tomb. In three days, He rose again, conquering death and the grave. As a result of the resurrection of Jesus, Paul declared in 1 Corinthians 15:55, "O Death, where is your sting? O Hades, where is your victory?"

The miraculous victory of Jesus over death and the grave is what sets Christianity apart from the other religions. Yes, other religious leaders have put forth some practical teaching, some of which follows the moral law of God, which is written on the hearts of man, yet all other religions are works based—how well you accomplish certain things or whether you can keep a certain moral code. None of them had leaders or God incarnate come and die for the people and then rise again. Again, why is the resurrection of Jesus fundamental to our faith? Paul laid it on the line in 1 Corinthians 15:14: "And if Christ is not risen, then our preaching is empty and your faith is also empty."

One more thing to notice in these first ten verses is that the risen Jesus first appeared to women who followed Him. Unlike Peter and the apostles, who fled when Jesus was arrested and didn't resurface until after He rose, these women remained faithful at every step. They stayed and watched Jesus die on the cross; they followed and observed His burial; they returned to the tomb to anoint His body; they entered the empty tomb and encountered angels who told them He had risen; and then they met the risen Jesus!

In fact, we read about it in Matthew 28:9–10, "And as they went to tell His disciples, behold, Jesus met them, saying, 'Rejoice!' So they came and held Him by the feet and worshiped Him. Then Jesus said to them, "Do not be afraid. Go and tell My brethren to go to Galilee, and there they will see Me." These faithful women relayed that amazing news to His apostles, who thought they were talking nonsense and didn't believe them. Yet these women became the "apostles to the Apostles." In a Jewish culture that dismissed the testimony of a woman as essentially worthless, Jesus rewarded their faithfulness, giving this circle of female followers the privilege and responsibility of being the first witnesses of Him as risen Lord.

But don't miss the big point: Jesus chose to reveal Himself as risen Lord beginning with these faithful women who had been with Him to the very end. It punctuates for me the fact that faithfulness to the Lord is rewarded with even more revelation of Jesus to us. If you want to experience more of Jesus, hang on to Him and hang in there with Him, be a faithful follower. A reward is in it, and the reward is the revelation of Jesus Himself!

Next, we see that the critics here conspired to somehow rationalize and cover up the fact that Jesus rose from the dead. The same ones who paid Judas to turn Jesus over then gave money to the eyewitnesses to cover up Jesus's resurrection. And the response of the opponents of truth is very revealing in confirming the truth.

Look at Matthew 28:11–13: "Now while they were going, behold, some of the guard came into the city and reported to the chief priests all the things that had happened. When they had assembled with the elders and consulted together, they gave a large sum of money to the soldiers, saying, 'Tell them, "His disciples came at night and stole Him away while we slept."'"

Now think about that for just a moment. If they were asleep, how would they know the disciples came and stole the body of Jesus? Let's continue in Matthew 28:14: "'And if this comes to the governor's ears, we will appease him and make you secure.'" It was a death sentence to be caught sleeping on the post. They would have neglected their duties that way. So they said, "Look, here's a lot of money. Go say this happened and we will take care of it if it comes to the governor's ear." Verses 15 says, "So they took the money and did as they were instructed; and this saying is commonly reported among the Jews until this day."

Then finally in this concluding chapter of Matthew's Gospel, we have the commissioning of the disciples. Look at verses 16–20:

> Then the eleven disciples went away into Galilee, to the mountain which Jesus had appointed for them. When they saw Him, they worshiped Him; but some doubted. And Jesus came and spoke to them, saying, "All authority has been given to Me in heaven and on earth. Go therefore and make disciples of all the nations, baptizing them in the name of the Father and of the Son and of the Holy Spirit, teaching them to observe all things that I have commanded you; and lo, I am with you always, even to the end of the age." Amen.

This is what we call the Great Commission. We are to make disciples, baptize disciples, and teach disciples the Word of God. It's handed down from one generation to the next. This is the mission of the church. Yet we are to go with the understanding that we operate in His power, under Christ who has ultimate authority. As Paul wrote in Philippians 2:8–11: "And being found in appearance as a man, He humbled Himself and became obedient to the point of death, even the death of the cross. Therefore God also has highly exalted Him and given Him the name which is above every name, that at the name of Jesus every knee should bow, of those in heaven, and of those on earth, and of those under the earth, and that every tongue should confess that Jesus Christ is Lord, to the glory of God the Father." Through the obedience of death on the cross, Jesus was given authority over heaven and over the earth.

Now, this does not mean there is no resistance to this authority in the present. Here's an analogy; it's limited, but I'll use it. The sheriff of a county is the chief law enforcement officer. He has all the authority needed to uphold the law. But that does not mean there are no criminals who violate the law. But as his deputies go out into the streets, they become evangelists, so to speak, for law and order. In other words, as we go, taking the Word of God and making disciples, we advance the kingdom of God under His delegated authority. But there will come a point when the Lord returns at His second coming, and His kingdom will be established universally and for eternity, based upon this authority that He was given.

In the meantime, there is a spiritual battle raging over the entire world, and you and I have been commissioned to go into this battle in the name of Jesus, to fight the forces of darkness. Our weapons are not carnal; they're spiritual. Our warfare is not physical; it is spiritual. The enemies are not physical enemies. But we're to do battle nonetheless. And what we are battling for is to see the souls of men, women, and children set free by the truth of the gospel of Jesus Christ. That is the mission of the church, and we have His delegated authority.

We have been commissioned by Jesus Christ if we have accepted Him as our Lord and our Savior. Consequently, we are to walk in obedience to Him and know that as we carry out His command to make disciples, baptize disciples, and teach disciples that the promise of Jesus is this: "I am with you always, even to the end of the age" (Matt. 28:20). That amazing promise is the bookend to the promise before His birth: "'they shall call His name Immanuel,' which is translated, 'God with us.'" From beginning to end, we have the risen Jesus's empowering and encouraging presence through the person of the Holy Spirit to accomplish His Great Commission. May He find us faithful!

Questions for Reflection and Discussion

1. After rolling away the stone, what did the angel of the Lord say to the women who came to Jesus's tomb on that Sunday morning (see vv. 1–8)?
2. What final directive or mission did Jesus give His disciples before He ascended into heaven (see vv. 16–20)?
   a. Make disciples
   b. Baptize disciples
   c. Teach disciples
   d. All of the above

Notes on Today's Bible Reading

Appendix 1:
Stand on the Word Bible Reading Plan

Visit frc.org/Bible for our chronological journey through the Bible that we call "Stand on the Word." We encourage you to spend time reading and studying the Bible because it is literally "God-breathed" (2 Tim. 3:16 NIV); it is God's very words to us. The Bible answers the big questions, such as, Why am I here? Where did I come from? Where am I going (life after death)? If God is good, why does evil and suffering exist? The Bible not only answers these big questions; it offers practical advice in areas such as, How can I deal with feelings of fear or anger or guilt? How can I forgive when I cannot forget? What should I look for in a spouse? How can I have a successful marriage? How can I be a good parent? What is my spiritual gift and place in the church? What is my stewardship responsibility as a citizen? We learned the verse in Bible school, "Your word is a lamp to my feet and a light to my path" (Ps. 119:105). God's Word shows us the way forward in any area of life and on every question we face.

The Stand on the Word Bible Reading Plan takes us through the Bible chronologically. In other words, each reading takes us through the Bible as events occurred in history as far as it is possible. Here is how it works for our family. At the same time each morning, whether I am at home, in Washington, or some foreign country, I send my wife and children a morning greeting along with a reminder of the passage for the day. The text includes two questions related to the reading. The questions are designed to help in content retention, serve as an accountability tool, and provide for discussion.

The two-year plan does not have a Sunday passage. Instead, it provides an outline for a family discussion that can be done on Sunday afternoon or evening. Our family has incorporated the discussion into our Sunday lunch, which follows a biblical model of life enriching conversations over a meal. The weekly discussion time begins with a spiritual leader asking each person individually for one or two insights or truths they gained from their reading during the week and how those truths apply to our lives. After everyone else shares, the father or group leader can lead a short discussion of one of the passages that was read during the week and how it applies to our lives here and now. It is also a time for them to ask questions.

By the way, you don't have to have all the answers. If you don't know, tell them so, then talk to your pastor or other trusted person with Bible knowledge. If your children start asking questions, that suggests they are thinking about what they are reading.

Reading God's Word will help you establish a fruitful walk with the God who made you and loves you. Whether you are single or married, this plan will enable you to lead your friends and family in daily reading God's Word. The added benefit is that you will all be reading the same text together. It will amaze you to see how God speaks sometimes in the same ways and at other times in different ways to each of you. Being on this journey together will build a spiritual synergy, a deep bond, and sense of unity and purpose like nothing else! Use it to impart the Word of life. Visit frc.org/Bible to sign up or simply download the Stand Firm App.

Appendix 2:
Prayer: Talking with God

Most Americans say they pray, but not as many pray the way Jesus did and taught His disciples to pray. Fewer, still, really know the power in prayer that God gave us to impact our families, communities, nation, and world. But prayer is our lifeline to God, our means of communicating with our heavenly Father. It develops our relationship—our friendship, fellowship, and intimacy—with Him. In prayer we experience God and are "filled with the Spirit" (Eph. 5:18–21). God uses the prayers of faithful men, women, boys, and girls to heal broken lives and strengthen families, churches, communities, and even nations. He uses our prayers to advance His kingdom on earth (Daniel 9; Acts 4:36)! He wants to so use all believers!

The Essence of Prayer

Prayer is simply talking with God—about anything and everything. He is our Maker, Father, Savior, Provider, and Counselor, our Master, Healer, Guide, and Friend. Christ died for our sins and rose from the dead to sit at the right hand of God the Father, where He is praying for us right now (Heb. 10:12). His Spirit now lives within us and helps us to pray (1 John 4:16).

The Priority of Prayer

Jesus spent time alone with God regularly drawing strength from the Father and seeking His will for every decision (Luke 6:12–13; 22:39–44). His disciples asked Jesus to teach them how to pray (Luke 11:1–13). The apostles knew that prayer and obedience were the keys to Christ's life and ministry and were determined to follow His example: "[W]e will devote ourselves to prayer and to the ministry of the word" (Acts 6:4 ESV). Too few American men pray today, even pastors and leaders! Yet strong praying men are the norm in Scripture. Our families, churches, and nation need men who will make prayer a priority today! (1 Tim. 2:8)

The Practice of Prayer

Scripture teaches, "Pray continually!" (1 Thess. 5:17 NIV); "Praying always" (Eph. 6:18); "Always pray and not give up" (Luke 18:1 NIV). Below are some helps to get you started. No one can beat the Lord's Prayer. It is an outline of key themes to guide our prayer lives:

> "Our Father in heaven,
> hallowed be your name.
> Your kingdom come,
> your will be done,
>   on earth as it is in heaven.
> Give us this day our daily bread,
> and forgive us our debts,
>   as we also have forgiven our debtors.

And lead us not into temptation,
but deliver us from evil." (Matt. 6:9–13 ESV)

In the book of Psalms and throughout Scripture, God has sprinkled prayers: patterns for us to learn from. Here is a simple, popular acronym to help jog our memories:

P-R-A-Y:

- *Praise:* Our Father in heaven, hallowed be your name.
- *Repent:* And forgive us our debts, as we also have forgiven our debtors.
- *Ask:* Give us this day our daily bread, and forgive us our debts, as we also have forgiven our debtors. And lead us not into temptation, but deliver us from evil.
- *Yield:* Your kingdom come, your will be done, on earth as it is in heaven.

Praying Through Scripture

God also talks to us. The Bible is His Word (2 Tim. 2:15; 3:16). Bible in hand, we should pray God's promises back to Him, and claim them for our families, our work, our finances, and our nation (1 Tim. 2:1–8; 1 John 5:14–15).

Scriptures to Pray as a Man: Joshua 1:8; 1 Timothy 3:1–15; 1 Chronicles 12:32; 1 Timothy 6:1–12; 1 Corinthians 16:13; Romans 12:1–21; Micah 6:8; John 4:24; Acts 2:38; 1 Kings 2:2; Husbands: Ephesians 5:25–28; Genesis 2:24; 1 Peter 3:7; Ephesians 4:26–27; Matthew 5:32; Proverbs 5:19; 1 Corinthians 6:18; Fathers: Deuteronomy 4:8–10; 11:18–21; Exodus 34:5–8; Psalm 127:3–5; Matthew 7:11; Ephesians 6:4; Proverbs 22:6; Luke 11:11–12; Hebrews 12:5–7

Scriptures to Pray as a Woman: Matthew 22:36–40; Proverbs 31:30; 1 Peter 3:1–3; Ephesians 5:26; Ephesians 4:15, 29; 1 Timothy 3:11; Ephesians 5:22, 24; 1 Peter 3:1–2; Philippians 4:10– 13; Philippians 2:3–4; Proverbs 31:12; 1 Corinthians 7:34; Titus 2:3–4; Titus 2:4–5; James 1:19; Ephesians 4:32; 1 Corinthians 7:1–5; Luke 2:37; Colossians 4:2; Proverbs 31:27; 1 Timothy 5:14

Scriptures to Pray for Your Children: Matthew 22:36–40; 2 Timothy 3:15; Psalm 97:10, 38:18; Proverbs 8:13; John 17:15, 10:10; Romans 12:9; Psalm 119:71; Hebrews 12:5–6; Daniel 1:17, 20; Proverbs 1:4; James 1:5; Romans 13:1; Ephesians 6:1–3; Hebrews 13:17; Proverbs 1:10–16, 13:20; 2 Corinthians 6:14–17; Deuteronomy 6; 1 Corinthians 6:18–20; Acts 24:16; 1 Timothy 1:19, 4:1–2; Titus 1:15–16; Psalm 23:4; Deuteronomy 10:12; Matthew 28:18–20; Ephesians 1:3, 4:29; Ephesians 1:16–19; Philippians 1:11; Colossians 1:9; Philippians 1:9–10

Developing Personal Prayer Habits

Rise early each day to pray with opened Bible. Daniel prayed three times daily. Pray whenever you can: as you drive, with your wife, with your children at dinner and before bedtime. You cannot pray too much!

Praying Together with Others

Pray with your spouse regularly. Make time for family prayer. Be part of your church prayer meeting or group. Christ said, "My house shall be called a house of prayer." The apostle Paul instructed Pastor Timothy (1 Tim. 2:1–8) to make prayer the first order of the church, saying prayer is key to peace in the nation. There is nothing like a Spirit-led prayer meeting with people who love the Lord! Praying women have been standing in the prayer gap for decades.

Every man must set his heart to become a praying man, lead his family in prayer, and be a strong contributor to the corporate prayer life of his church. We must be leaders in praying for our morally and spiritually troubled, divided nation—and for our national leaders. American Christians simply must respond to God's promise: "If My people who are called by My name will humble themselves, and pray and seek My face, and turn from their wicked ways, then I will hear from heaven, and will forgive their sin and heal their land" (2 Chron. 7:14).

Prayer As Warfare

Jesus described the enemy, the devil, as a thief whose mission is "to steal, and to kill, and to destroy" (John 10:10). Demonic forces are at war against everything good in you, your family, your church, your community, America, and every nation (Eph. 6:10–20).

The devil and his minions are out to thwart the kingdom of God and eliminate righteousness wherever he can. He hates God, hates people, and will use spiritually ignorant and deceived men, women, boys, and girls to do his bidding. Men of God today, like the sons of Issachar in ancient Israel, need to understand the times and know what the church and our nation must do (1 Chron. 12:32). We must pull down Satan's strongholds, wrestle for our families, and use Spirit-led prayer and wisdom to help guide our churches and communities to prevail against the evil onslaught against us (2 Cor. 10:3–5). This is the war of the ages and it is real.

Finally, Determine to Become a Person of Prayer

No matter how long you have been a Christian and may have neglected prayer up until now, you can become a person of prayer starting today. If you have missed the mark, it is not too late. Call upon the Lord, ask His help, and proceed with His guidance. *O Lord, make me a praying person; make me a prayer warrior! In Jesus's name, amen!*

Appendix 3:
How to Share Your Faith

Recent polling from Lifeway Research shows that "only 3 in 10 unchurched Americans (29%) say a Christian has ever shared with them one-on-one how a person becomes a Christian."[12]

Even less are successful in helping someone make a decision to follow Christ. Maybe that is why this whole notion of sharing your faith is so intimidating for many. However, it does not have to be. The best place to start is with your story. Some call it a testimony. In a courtroom, testimony is relied on as part of the evidence in a case. As you are telling your story, you are presenting evidence for how Christ has changed your life for the better. If you are speaking with another man about your faith, think in terms of telling your story in three parts:

1. Your life before you became a follower of Christ.
2. Your encounter with Christ and your decision to follow him as your Savior and Lord.
3. Your life since becoming as a follower of Christ.

The great apostle Paul told his faith story numerous times—several of them are recorded in the Bible. You'll notice these same three parts in Acts 22.

1. Life Before Christ

First of all, notice what Paul said about his life before Christ:

> "I am a Jew, born in Tarsus in Cilicia, but brought up in this city, educated at the feet of Gamaliel according to the strict manner of the law of our fathers, being zealous for God as all of you are this day. I persecuted this Way to the death, binding and delivering to prison both men and women, as the high priest and the whole council of elders can bear me witness. From them I received letters to the brothers, and I journeyed toward Damascus to take those also who were there and bring them in bonds to Jerusalem to be punished." (Acts 22:3–5 ESV)

If there was ever a Jew who was steeped in religion, that Jew was Paul. His religious trophy case was filled to overflowing (v. 3). Over in Philippians 3, he pulled out and dusted off several of them. Then he described his radical commitment to his religion to the point of persecuting followers of Christ (vv. 4–5). Take time to write out what you remember about your life before your life-changing encounter with Christ. Be brief and to the point:

2. Encounter with Christ

Paul not only told about his life before Christ, but then he shared his life-changing encounter with Christ:

> "As I was on my way and drew near to Damascus, about noon a great light from heaven suddenly shone around me. And I fell to the ground and heard a voice saying to me, 'Saul, Saul, why are you persecuting me?' And I answered, 'Who are you, Lord?' And he said to me, 'I am Jesus of Nazareth, whom you are persecuting.' Now those who were with me saw the light but did not understand the voice of the one who was speaking to me." (Acts 22:6–9 ESV)

Notice Paul said in verse 9: "Who are you, Lord?" He was told by a heavenly voice: "I am Jesus of Nazareth, whom you are persecuting." What an amazing encounter! Obviously, most people don't get blinded by a light or hear voices from heaven. However, your story of your encounter with Christ is unique, and no doubt it was (and hopefully still is) a powerful experience for you. Take time to write out your encounter with Christ and how you came to make the decision to follow him as Savior and Lord, but don't rush it. Tell what happened in detail:

3. Life-Change After Christ

Paul then began to tell about the changes in his life after his encounter with Christ:

> "And I said, 'What shall I do, Lord?' And the Lord said to me, 'Rise, and go into Damascus, and there you will be told all that is appointed for you to do.' And since I could not see because of the brightness of that light, I was led by the hand by those who were with me, and came into Damascus.
>
> "And one Ananias, a devout man according to the law, well spoken of by all the Jews who lived there, came to me,

> and standing by me said to me, 'Brother Saul, receive your sight.' And at that very hour I received my sight and saw him. And he said, 'The God of our fathers appointed you to know his will, to see the Righteous One and to hear a voice from his mouth; for you will be a witness for him to everyone of what you have seen and heard. And now why do you wait? Rise and be baptized and wash away your sins, calling on his name.'" (Acts 22:10–16 ESV)

In verse 10, Paul asked, basically, "Lord, what next?" and the risen Christ told him, "You will be told all that is appointed for you to do." And then Ananias, another disciple of Jesus, communicated Paul's assignment in verses 13–16, which was basically to give his testimony and tell his story "to all people." Obviously, Paul accepted his assignment and went on to become one of the greatest leaders in the history of the Christian faith, going on missionary journeys, leading multitudes to faith in Jesus, planting churches, ordaining leaders, even giving his testimony to officials in Rome, which was the capital of the ancient world. He also experienced persecution, imprisonment, and finally death for his faith. Again, Paul's story can be intimidating, but it doesn't need to be. Just think about how your life has changed since you began following Christ. Write down some of your thoughts. Remember, you are trying to offer compelling evidence.

Having read how Paul told his faith story, use the outline above and write out yours. Once you have written it, read through it and prayerfully edit it. After you feel good about it, practice sharing it with another trusted and seasoned believer, preferably someone who has successfully helped lead someone else to faith in Christ. Then you may want to go back and edit it again as you may have thought about a better way to communicate it. Finally, pray for God to open a door of opportunity to share your faith story with someone. Pray that the Holy Spirit will prepare the way for you and do only what He can do. At the end of our best efforts to share Christ, it is still up to God and the individual.

Appendix 4:
The Solution to Our Greatest Challenge

What is the greatest challenge facing families and the church today? It is a lack of a biblical worldview. A worldview is the lens through which we view life and the world around us. Having a biblical worldview means the Bible is our lens. Everything in life is filtered through and viewed from a biblical perspective. The problem is that very few can truthfully claim that the Bible is their authoritative point of reference for what they value and how they behave. In fact, renowned researcher Dr. George Barna has found through extensive surveys measuring against seven core principles foundational to a biblical worldview that only 4 percent of Americans actually view their world through a biblical lens.[13]

What complicates matters is that our worldview is largely developed during childhood. Dr. Barna, Senior Research Fellow for the Center for Biblical Worldview at Family Research Council, has determined that a person's worldview is primarily established between the ages of fifteen months and thirteen years.[14] The problem is that the vast majority of kids reach their teenage years without a biblical worldview.

Here is more definitive evidence. The Nehemiah Institute, founded in 1986, is on a mission to provide worldview assessment to youth in Christian homes associated with Christian schools, homeschool associations, and church youth groups.[15] Called "PEERS," it is the only professionally validated worldview assessment available that I'm aware of. It's fairly comprehensive with seventy test items, fourteen in each category, that the kids take, and it breaks down the results. All the students who take the test fall into four broad categories of worldview:

- Biblical Theism (meaning a Biblical Worldview)
- Moderate Christian
- Secular Humanism
- Socialism

Keep in mind that this is only self-described Christian kids in Christian schools, youth groups, or homeschool. Based on almost forty years of results, PEERS testing shows that a majority of youth from Christian homes are abandoning a biblical worldview and biblical theism in favor of a secular worldview, if not a socialist worldview. When PEERS was first launched in the 1980s, the majority of youth from Christian homes scored mainly in either the moderate Christian worldview or biblical theism worldview. Today, the same demographic shows more than 90 percent of Christian youth scoring in the secular humanism category using the exact same questions that were used in the 1980s, and less than 3 percent are scoring in the biblical theism category. Again, these are kids in Christian schools, church youth groups, and homeschool.

Consequently, this is arguably the single greatest problem facing families and the church in America today, and why we must teach our children. We should not be surprised by these numbers when we are outsourcing the education of our children to people who, for the most part, not only don't have a biblical worldview, but many have an antibiblical worldview. This is why Scripture tells parents that we are primarily responsible to talk about God's Word with our children "when you sit in your house, when you walk by the way, when you lie down, and when you rise up" (see Deut. 6:4–9). We should be teaching our children and our grandchildren the Word of God and its application to our world. Yet when we outsource that to someone else, we see sad results. Of course, we must factor in that it is not simply what's happening in a classroom; it is also shaped by what they're listening to, watching, and engaging with on social media, etc. Furthermore, parents cannot give what they don't have. So, if parents don't have a biblical worldview, they cannot give their children a biblical worldview. And you cannot get a biblical worldview unless you are regularly reading the Word of God.

That brings me to the proposed solution. Again, to gain a biblical worldview, a person must be regularly reading and studying and applying the Word of God. That is what spurred me to develop our Stand on the Word Bible Reading Plan. It is a two-year, chronologically prioritized Bible reading plan that takes ten to fifteen minutes a day of reading, six days a week, Monday through Saturday. On Sunday, there's no reading because it's a discussion day for the family, a day to reflect on what we have read over the previous week and share how God is speaking to us.

This Bible reading plan came about a number of years ago when I was looking for a devotional book for our family—something that would allow five children, ranging from two to eighteen years old, to have a conversation. A lot of people send me books and devotionals with an interest in being a guest on *Washington Watch* to talk about their book, so I had a good handle on pretty much everything that was out there. I looked for six months—read them, studied them, went through them myself—and couldn't find anything that I felt would work. Finally, the Holy Spirit said, "Try the Bible."

So, we began with a couple of books from the New Testament, letters of Paul, and then I began to look at how we could take the entire Bible, breaking it up into a two-year reading plan as opposed to a one-year plan. The latter, for most people, becomes like a speed reading course where not much gets absorbed. However, with the two-year plan, everyone can read it in bite-sized chunks, and each day comes with two questions for reflection. The questions also served as an accountability to gauge who in the family was reading the chapters. And wherever I might be in the world, I would set my clock so that at 7 a.m. central time I would text my family the reading for the day and the two associated questions.

Then on Sunday, after lunch, we would have a conversation about the chapters we read that week and how it applies to the world in which we live. Our weekly time together as a family became the highlight of my week. Here is a suggested template for your gathering:

- Opening Prayer – Praise and a brief prayer for spiritual insight and unity.
- Recap – Briefly summarize the chapters covered that week.
- Discussion Questions – Use open-ended, age-appropriate prompts to spark meaningful worldview conversations. Here are some suggestions:
    1. Most meaningful passage that spoke to you personally?

2. Insights gained about God: Who He is, What He values and expects, How He works?
3. Applications that we can make from the Word to what is happening in the world?
4. How would God have you apply His truth to your life personally?

- Action Steps – Encourage each family member to share a personal takeaway or action step for living the truth revealed in God's Word.
- Closing Prayer – Conclude by praising God for how He has revealed Himself, His purposes, and His ways, and by praying for His help in living in the light of His truth and sharing it with others during the week ahead.

For our family, these Sunday gatherings were nearly as meaningful as a church worship service! Now that nearly all of our kids are grown and some are establishing their own families, I pray they will do the same with their children as God gives them. But that was the strategy we used, and God has blessed it.

That Sunday debrief time is a key part of this strategy to develop a biblical worldview. The inspiration for it came about from a trip I took a number of years ago to Israel and attended a Shabbat dinner with a family. I was fascinated with the conversation around the dinner table, talking about the application of God's Word to the world in which we live. And I thought, "You know, that is what's missing, a conversation to help develop a biblical worldview." I had one child who was in college at the time. So, on Sunday we would dissect what they were being taught (because it was a secular college) and equip them to counter those arguments that they were hearing. We were honing her biblical worldview.

The bottom line here is that it is vitally important that we are intentional about cultivating a biblical worldview in our family members as well as with church members. I believe that reading the Bible daily, with a daily touch-of-base about the reading, followed by an extended weekend conversation can provide the solution to the challenge of making sure our families and our churches develop a biblical worldview. I pray you will join us on this Stand on the Word journey through the Bible. Visit frc.org/Bible to sign up or simply download the Stand Firm app.

Notes

1. https://today.yougov.com/health/articles/51527–what-ameri cans-think-about-home-dna-tests-poll.

2. Lexie Pelchen, "Moving Statistics and Trends for 2025," Forbes, April 24, 2024, https://www.forbes.com/home-improvement/moving -services/annual-moving-trend-forecast/.

3. David Brown, "Gospel According to Matthew" in Robert Jamieson, A. R. Fausset, and David Brown, *A Commentary, Critical, Practical, and Explanatory on the Old and New Testaments*, 4 vols., (Harrington, DE: Delmarva Publications, 2013), 3:81

4. Brown, "Gospel According to Matthew," *A Commentary*, 3:100.

5. Roy P. Basler, ed., *The Collected Works of Abraham Lincoln*, 9 vols. (Rutgers University Press, 1953), 2:461.

6. Abraham Lincoln, "Address at Gettysburg," delivered on November 19, 1863, as found in Basler, *The Collected Works of Abraham Lincoln*, 7:22.

7. Max Farrand, ed., *The Records of the Federal Convention of 1787*, 3 vols. (Yale University Press, 1911), 3:85.

8. Samuel Adams, *The Writings of Samuel Adams*, Harry Alonzo Cushing, ed. (G. P. Putnam's Sons, 1907), 4:256, originally in the Boston Gazette, April 16, 1781.

9. John Jay, *The Correspondence and Public Papers of John Jay*, Henry P. Johnston, ed. (G. P. Putnam's Sons, 1890), 4:365.

10. Stanford University, The Martin Luther King, Jr. Research and Education Institute, Draft of Chapter VI, "A Knock at Midnight," https://kinginstitute.stanford.edu/king-papers/documents/draft-chapter-vi-knock-midnight.

11. David Ramsay, *An Eulogium upon Benjamin Rush, M. D.* (Bradford and Inskeep, 1813), 103.

12. https://research.lifeway.com/2021/09/09/christians-dont-share-faith-with-unchurched-friends/

13. Tracy Munsil, "Barna, CRC: Widespread Worldview Confusion Grows as Americans Redefine God," Arizona Christian University, February 18, 2025, https://www.arizonachristian.edu/2025/02/18/awvi-2025_01_most-americans-believe-in-a-supreme-power-but-not-the-god-of-the-bible/.

14. Tracy Munsil, "Most US Kids Ages 8-12 Lack Biblical 'Cornerstones,' Research Says," Arizona Christian University, October 11, 2023, https://www.arizonachristian.edu/2023/10/11/most-us-kids-ages-8-12-lack-biblical-cornerstones/.

15. https://www.worldviewcheckup.org/.

Other Study Guides Available from
Fidelis Publishing and Family Research Council

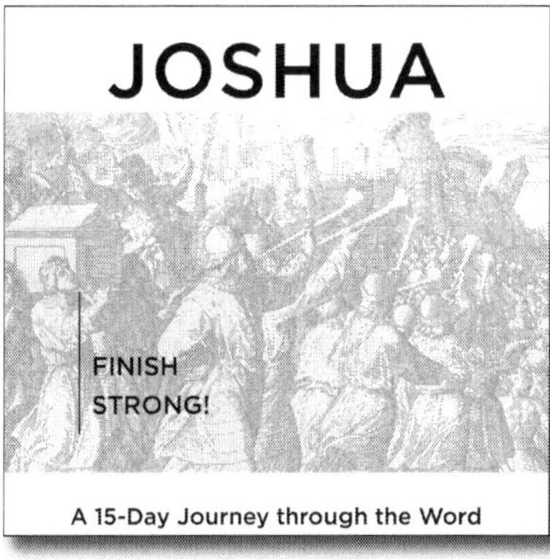

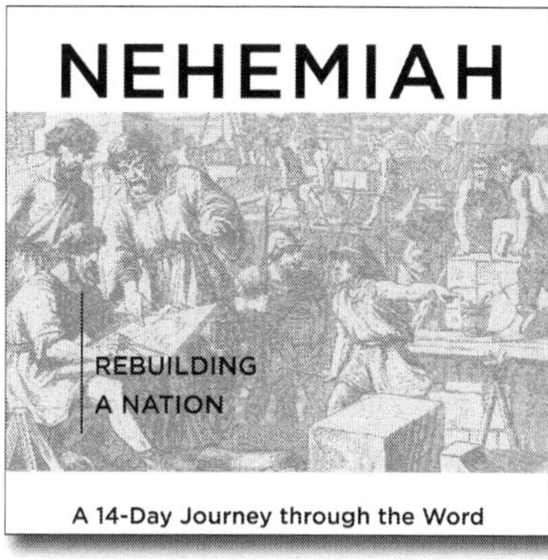

STAND on the WORD

Joshua: Finish Strong! ISBN: 9781956454802
Nehemiah: Rebuilding a Nation ISBN: 9781956454468
Jeremiah: Courage in a Cancel Culture ISBN: 9781956454369
Daniel: Visions and Valor ISBN: 9798992418651
Ephesians: Keep Standing! ISBN: 9781956454659

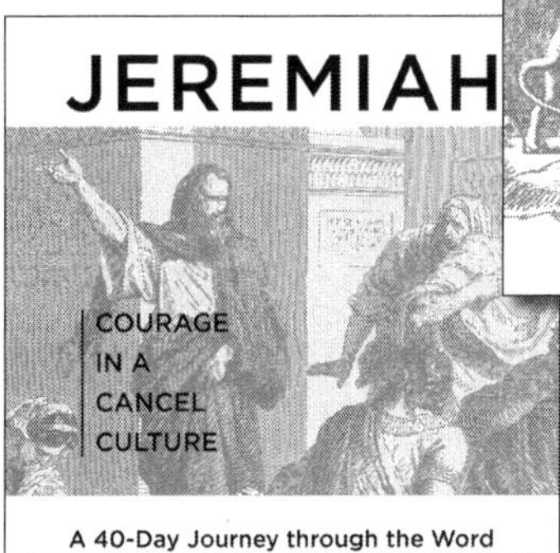

Also from Fidelis Publishing and Family Research Council

STAND on the WORD Journals

Volume 1
ISBN: 9781956454758

Volume 2
ISBN: 9781956454871